AF316665

These Pearls are dedicated to all the gems in my jewelry box.

To my onyx stones, the ancestors assigned to this bloodline. My Mother and Father have all been promoted to the position of guardian angel & my "Papa" for stepping up and extending my "lifeline." The summation of their value in my circle of life has allowed me to draw on their wells of wisdom, encouragement, strength, shoulders to lean on, and arms to hold me. Their intercessory prayers on my life are still a sweet fragrance, even now being received and answered by the Lord.

To my "Double Diamonds" – My son, Jaimel, and daughter, Bracha – my prayers and tears for them unto GOD have formed the hinges of my jewelry box. They have enriched me with rubies of grandaughters, sapphire great-granddaughters, jasper grandsons, and a great-grandson, hyacinth.

The opulence of the coral representing the rest of the jewels embedded in this jewelry box are the blended and extended sons and daughters that GOD has favored me to cover, like the Amethyst that wards off evil, warning against the drunkenness of vain & unprofitable ambitions.

My life with them is the process that pushes me
toward my purpose, the wind beneath my wings, and
the GOD-given strength that keeps me grounded and
focused on my becoming.

ONE LOVE,

NaNa

My Cup Runneth Over

NaNa's Pearls of Wisdom

Naomi K. Pettiford

Jaimel D. Hill

#DBWT

Contents

Dedication **ii**
Quick Note To The Reader **ix**
Opening Prayer **xi**

Pearl **1**

The 1st Pearl **7**

The 2nd Pearl **18**

The 3rd Pearl **27**

The 4th Pearl **37**

The 5th Pearl **44**

The 6th Pearl **51**

The 7th Pearl **57**

The 8th Pearl **64**

The 9th Pearl **71**

The 10th Pearl **80**

Contents

The 11th Pearl 92

The 12th Pearl 106

The 13th Pearl 114

The 14th Pearl 125

The 15th Pearl 143

The 16th Pearl 153

Closing Prayer 165
Call To Action 167
Meet Your Author 170
Appendix 173

quick note to the reader

Welcome to this enlightening book filled with wisdom and spiritual insight. As you read, remember that the book's value lies in thoroughly absorbing its lessons and messages. Each gem presented here is not merely a fleeting thought but a profound weekly lesson waiting to be explored at the beginning of each week.

Brief Bible studies accompany each message throughout these pages, offering more profound insights into Scripture's timeless truths. These studies will serve as guiding lights, illuminating the path to greater understanding and spiritual growth.

But the journey doesn't end with reading alone. You'll also find a week's worth of daily activities, each designed to help you apply the lessons learned practically to your daily life. From reflection exercises to acts of kindness, each activity is an opportunity to deepen your connection with the divine and live out the principles shared in this book.

Finally, after each week's activities, you'll discover journal questions to ponder and explore further. So grab a pen, because these questions invite introspection and self-discovery, allowing you to go deeper into the teachings and uncover their significance. So, as you turn the pages of this book, remember to engage fully with each lesson, activity, and question. Only through active participation and reflection can you realize the true transformational power of these gems of wisdom.

Opening Prayer

Most gracious and most merciful God,

We prostrate at your throne of mercy, supplicating to you from the sacred space of our hearts. We come before You with humble hearts, seeking Your divine guidance and wisdom. We stand on the shoulders of giants, inspired by the faith and resilience of those who have come before us.

We invoke the spirit of perseverance and strength that has carried generations through trials and tribulations, trusting in Your unfailing love and grace.

We recall the words of our ancestors, whose prayers echoed through the halls of history, shaping our collective travels with unwavering faith and conviction.

Lord, as we venture on this expedition through NaNa's Pearls of Wisdom, we ask for Your divine presence to illuminate our path and grant us clarity of mind and purity of heart.

May the words penned within these pages be a source of inspiration and transformation, guiding us toward a more profound understanding and spiritual growth.

Opening Prayer

We lift the voices of those who have walked before us, whose prayers continue to echo in the chambers of eternity, reminding us of the power of faith and the triumph of the human spirit.

We honor their legacy as we seek to embrace the challenges and opportunities that lie ahead, knowing that all things are possible with You.

We praise You, O Lord, through these pages of faith and discovery; we glorify Your name with every word, sentence, and paragraph.

As we turn these pages, we seek Your divine wisdom and guidance, knowing that You are the author of our lives and the source of all truth.

As we envelop ourselves in the mysteries of Your Word, we ask that Your presence fill these pages with Your light and Your love.

May Your grace be our constant companion and guide us through the twists and turns of life and the unknown.

We praise You, O Lord, and thank You for the opportunity to draw closer to You with each page turn. May Your name be lifted high in every word we read, and may Your glory shine forth from every page we turn.

O Gracious Almighty God, We humble ourselves by offering our words and skillful strokes of our pens, and we present this literary work before You, acknowledging Your sovereignty and majesty.

May every utterance of our mouths and every sound of words You've gifted us to speak be a sacrifice acceptable unto Your honor and pleasure.

With conviction in our hearts and minds, we declare that no one else is worthy of worship, and we offer thanks and honor to You through our skills and talents.

As we read this book, may it be a vessel for Your will, a ministry of literature to witness and fellowship. May the words penned within these pages be guided by Your divine inspiration,

And may they serve as beacons of light, leading others to You. Grant us the wisdom and discernment to convey Your truth with clarity and grace,

And may the message within these works resonate with hearts and minds, drawing souls closer to You.

Bless our endeavors, O Lord, and may this book bring glory to Your holy name as we seek to fulfill Your purpose and share Your love with the world.

In Your mercy and grace, we place our trust. And in Your infinite wisdom, we find our strength. In the name of Jesus, our Savior and Redeemer, we offer this prayer with gratitude and anticipation. For Yours is the kingdom, the power, and the glory, now and forevermore.

Amen.

My Cup Runneth Over

Pearl

A pearl is a lustrous, round gemstone produced within the soft tissue of a living mollusk, typically an oyster or a mussel. It is formed when an irritant, such as a grain of sand or a parasite, becomes trapped within the mollusk's shell. In response to this irritant, the mollusk secretes layers of nacre, a crystalline substance known as mother-of-pearl, around the intruder to protect itself.

Over time, as layer upon layer of nacre is deposited, a pearl is gradually formed. The process of pearl formation can take several years, depending on factors such as the size of the mollusk and the conditions of its environment. The result is a smooth, spherical gemstone with a lustrous sheen, valued for its beauty and rarity.

Pearls come in various colors, from white and cream to pink, black, and even iridescent shades. They are prized for their elegance and versatility, often used in jewelry-making to create necklaces, earrings, bracelets, and other adornments.

Beyond their physical beauty, pearls carry symbolic and spiritual significance in many cultures worldwide. They are often associated with purity, wisdom, and spiritual enlightenment and are given as gifts to mark special occasions such as weddings, anniversaries, and religious ceremonies.

For centuries, pearls have held a special place in human culture and spirituality. They are revered for their beauty, rarity, and symbolic significance. Beyond their physical allure, pearls carry profound spiritual and esoteric meanings that resonate deeply with the human soul.

Metaphorical Origins and Allegory:

The journey of a pearl begins in the depths of the ocean, where it is formed through transformation and growth. Similarly, the human soul undergoes its journey of development and enlightenment, emerging from the depths of darkness into the light of spiritual awareness.

In many spiritual traditions, pearls symbolize purity, wisdom, and enlightenment. Just as the oyster transforms an irritant into a radiant pearl, so does the soul transform adversity and challenges into knowledge and insight. The journey of the pearl serves as an allegory for the transformative power of perseverance, resilience, and inner growth.

Symbolism and Spiritual Significance:

Pearls are often associated with the divine feminine energy and are seen as symbols of the Goddess in many cultures. In Hindu mythology, the Goddess Lakshmi, the embodiment of wealth, prosperity, and beauty, is often depicted adorned with pearls. In Christianity, pearls are mentioned in the Bible as symbols of spiritual wealth and the kingdom of heaven.

Furthermore, pearls are considered sacred gems in various spiritual practices, including Buddhism and Taoism. They represent the Eightfold Path and the Tao, symbolizing the journey to spiritual enlightenment and inner peace.

Esoteric Meaning and Spiritual Wisdom:

Beyond their physical beauty, pearls carry esoteric meanings that speak to the more profound mysteries of existence. In mystical traditions, pearls are associated with the third eye chakra, the center of intuition, insight, and spiritual vision. They are believed to enhance psychic abilities and facilitate spiritual growth and enlightenment.

Moreover, pearls are often used in spiritual rituals and ceremonies to invoke divine blessings and protection. They are seen as conduits for divine energy, connecting the wearer to higher realms of consciousness and spiritual wisdom.

Life, Knowledge, Wisdom, and Success:

In the context of life, knowledge, wisdom, and success, pearls serve as powerful symbols of transformation and personal growth. Just as the oyster transforms a grain of sand into a precious gem, so too can adversity and challenges shape us into wiser, more resilient individuals.

Pearls remind us that true success is not measured by material wealth or external achievements but by the depth of our inner wisdom and the purity of our intentions. They encourage us to embrace the journey of self-discovery and spiritual enlightenment, knowing that true wealth lies in the treasures of the soul.

In essence, pearls' spiritual relevance and symbolism invite us to embark on a journey of inner exploration and transformation guided by the wisdom of the ages and the light of spiritual truth. They remind us that the potential for greatness lies within our being, waiting to be unearthed and polished into radiant pearls of spiritual enlightenment.

Pearls: Symbols of Love and Family

In the rich tapestry of symbolism surrounding pearls, their association with love and family is a testament to their profound significance in human relationships and connections. The journey of a pearl, from its inception as an irritant within an oyster to its emergence as a lustrous gem, mirrors the evolution of love and family bonds. Like the nurturing environment of the oyster that transforms the irritant into a thing of beauty, the love and care within a family can transform challenges and hardships into opportunities for growth and connection.

Symbolism of Love:

Pearls are often seen as symbols of love, purity, and devotion. In many cultures, they are given as tokens of affection and commitment, representing the deep bonds of love shared between partners. Pearls' luminescence reflects the radiance of love, illuminating the path of those who cherish and honor its presence in their lives.

Within the family context, pearls remind us of the enduring love that binds parents, children, siblings, and relatives together. They symbolize the precious moments shared, sacrifices, and unwavering support given in times of joy and sorrow. Like pearls on a necklace, family members are united by the common thread of love, forming a beautiful and intricate tapestry of relationships.

Nurturing and Growth:

Just as an oyster nurtures a pearl within its protective shell, families provide a nurturing environment for their members to thrive and grow. Within the embrace of family love, individuals are encouraged to explore their talents, pursue their passions, and overcome obstacles with resilience and strength.

Moreover, pearls symbolize the growth and maturation of familial relationships over time. Like pearls, families evolve and change, adapting to life's challenges while remaining rooted in the values and traditions that bind them together. Each member contributes to the family's collective wisdom and strength, adding depth and richness to the tapestry of their shared experiences.

Legacy and Heritage:

Pearls also carry the weight of heritage and legacy within family lineages. Passed down from generation to generation, they serve as tangible reminders of ancestors' love, wisdom, and traditions. As pearls retain their luster over time, so do the values and memories instilled within family structures, shaping the identities and futures of future generations.

Pearls are timeless symbols of love and family, encapsulating human connections' beauty, strength, and resilience. In the embrace of family love, individuals find solace, support, and belonging, nurturing the seeds of their dreams and aspirations while honoring the bonds that unite them.

We hope you enjoy this book, a gift of pearls of wisdom offered to you with love and sincerity. As each pearl is unique and precious, so are the insights within these pages. May they guide your journey of growth and self-discovery, illuminating the path to deeper understanding and fulfillment.

We extend this offering to you in the spirit of generosity and goodwill, trusting that it will resonate with your heart and soul. May these pearls of wisdom enrich your life and inspire you to embrace the beauty and complexity of the human experience. As you delve into the depths of these pages, may you find solace, inspiration, and enlightenment.

With gratitude and blessings,

Jaimel D. Hill

The 1st Pearl

Written in December 2020

It is almost 2021. Did I say enough, do enough, love enough, pray enough?

My answer: Whatever the amount, it's a "wrap" for 2020 – but Lord's will my cup "starteth" over for 2021. Being accountable to me, for me: I will endeavor to "Lift" my voice, "Pump up" my doing; "Magnify" the agape (unconditional) love in me; & "Pray without ceasing" for GOD's love; grace; mercy; healing; salvation; redemption; provision; protection; "sound" counsel; favor & for HIS Spirit to be the world's "spiritual stimulus." This is not a New Year's resolution but a New Life revelation. According to your measure of faith, let it be so unto you.

HE STILL WORKS MIRACLES! I LOVE YOU TO JESUS!

A New Life Revelation for the New Year
(written in 2021)

As we stand on the threshold of a new year, the question that often lingers is, "Did I say enough, do, love enough, pray enough in the year that just passed?" This question resonates with all of us, for we yearn to live lives of purpose, meaning, and impact. The passage of time offers us a moment to reflect, recalibrate, and renew our commitment to a well-lived life.

In the words of our dear friend, "Whatever the amount, it's a 'wrap' for 2020." Indeed, 2020 presented us with challenges and triumphs, joys and sorrows, but now, by the grace of the Almighty, we find ourselves on the cusp of a new beginning, a new chapter in the book of our lives. It is a chapter that we have the power to write, and with the guidance of the Lord, we can script a story of redemption, growth, and love.

In this new year, let us resolve to be accountable to ourselves, for ourselves. Let us take a cue from the wisdom of the ages and pledge to "Lift" our voices in praise, to "Pump up" our actions with purpose, to "Magnify" the agape love, the selfless and unconditional love, that resides within our hearts, and to "Pray without ceasing" for God's boundless love, grace, mercy, healing, salvation, redemption, provision, protection, and "sound" counsel, which refers to God's wise and righteous advice.

But this is not merely a set of New Year's resolutions but a profound revelation for a New Life. It is an awakening to the boundless potential within each of us. As we embark on this new journey, remember that it is not about the quantity but the quality of our actions, the size and sincerity of our love, and the frequency but the fervor of our prayers.

Our dear friend reminds us, "According to your measure of faith, let it be so unto you." This means that our faith, though it may start small, can move mountains, change lives, and transform our hearts. As we step into this new year, let us nurture and cultivate our faith, for it is the catalyst for change, the spark of hope, and the key to unlocking the blessings God has in store for us.

Let us be vessels of God's love, grace, and mercy, shining beacons of hope in a world that often seems lost and weary. Let us be the hands and feet of Jesus, extending compassion and kindness to all we encounter. Let us be fervent in our prayers, seeking our blessings and interceding for the needs of others so that God's love may flow through us to touch lives and transform souls.

Be blessed with spiritual insights and wisdom that transcend time and resonate deeply within our souls. They remind us that our journey is not defined by the past but by our choices today and the faith we hold in our hearts. As we step into 2021, let us do so with a renewed sense of purpose, a heart filled with love, and a commitment to pray without ceasing.

Now that 2024 is upon us, we must recognize the significance of each passing year in our lives. Time is a precious gift; with every new year, we can reflect on our past and chart a course for our future. While we may not have gathered in a physical event, our collective journey through life's chapters brings us together, sharing wisdom, experiences, and aspirations.

In the pages before us, we've already explored the profound message of accountability, faith, and the power of prayer. These timeless truths resonate deeply within our souls, guiding us toward growth and spiritual development. Now, as we look ahead to 2024, let us delve further into the wisdom that can illuminate our way forward. Life is a continuous journey of growth and self-discovery. Each day offers us a new opportunity to embrace the fullness of our potential, love unconditionally, and positively impact the world around us. This year, let us deepen our commitment to these ideals.

First and foremost, let us embrace the power of love. Love is not merely an emotion but a force that can transform lives. It transcends boundaries, bridges divides, and heals wounds. In 2024, let us strive to love more deeply, extend kindness to those around us, and comfort and support those in need.

Moreover, let us remember the significance of our actions. Each day presents us with choices, and it is through these choices that we shape our destinies. In the year ahead, let us act with intention, purpose, and commitment to positively impact. Let our actions reflect our values and a testament to our faith.

Faith, as we know, has the power to move mountains. It is the unwavering belief in the goodness of God and the potential within ourselves. In 2024, let us nurture our faith, for it is the foundation upon which our lives are built. Let us trust in God's plan, even in the face of uncertainty, and let our faith be a source of strength and resilience.

In this life journey, we must also recognize the importance of perseverance. Challenges will undoubtedly arise, but our determination to overcome them defines our character. Let us approach adversity with unwavering resolve, knowing we will grow stronger through these trials.

Lastly, let us always remember the power of community and unity. We are all on this journey together, and our collective efforts can bring about meaningful change. In 2024, let us unite as a community, supporting one another, lifting each other, and working towards a world that reflects the love, grace, and mercy we hold dear. As we embark on this new chapter, may our hearts be open to the blessings that await us, and may we be instruments of peace, hope, and love in a world that so desperately needs it. 2024 is an opportunity for growth, transformation, and living out the timeless wisdom we've discovered on this journey.

May God's guidance light our path, His love fill our hearts, and His grace sustain us throughout this new year. With faith, love, and unwavering commitment, let us move forward into 2024, ready to embrace the adventure that awaits. Allowing God's word to be our guiding light, His grace our strength, and His mercy our refuge in the days and weeks to come. And may His Spirit be the world's "spiritual stimulus," igniting a revival of faith, hope, and love in the hearts of all.

We pray in the name of the Father, the Son, and the Holy Spirit.

Amen.

Much Love, NaNa

By incorporating these daily activities into your life, you can embark on a transformative journey in 2024, deepening your faith, spreading love, and living a purposeful life guided by the wisdom and insights from our shared journey. May each day bring you closer to the path of love, grace, and fulfillment God has prepared for you.

Day 1: Embrace Unconditional Love: Today and each day, take a moment to meditate on unconditional love. Reflect on God's boundless love for us and our love for one another. Make it a point to express love to someone today, whether through a kind word, a thoughtful gesture, or a simple act of service.

Day 2: Set Purposeful Intentions: Start your day by setting clear intentions for how you want to live out your faith and values. Write down specific actions you can take to impact others positively here. Throughout the day, consciously choose actions that align with these intentions.

Day 3: Strengthen Your Faith: Devote time to nurturing your faith. Read a scripture passage or a spiritual text that resonates with you. Spend time in prayer, asking God for guidance, wisdom, and the strength to face challenges that may arise.

Day 4: Acts of Kindness: Challenge yourself to perform at least one intentional act of kindness daily. It can be as simple as listening to a friend in need, helping a neighbor, or donating to a charitable cause. These acts of kindness will reflect God's love in your daily life.

Day 5: Face Adversity with Resilience: Embrace adversity with unwavering resolve and faith. When faced with challenges, remind yourself that God is with your thoughts and feelings about overcoming difficulties and reaffirm your commitment to persevere.

Day 6: Foster Community and Unity: Reach out to a fellow believer or a friend in your community. Share your journey, your challenges, and your successes. Strengthen your bonds with others in your faith community, offering support, encouragement, and prayer when needed.

Day 7: Reflect and Plan: Reflect on your progress today. Evaluate how well you've embodied the principles of accountability, faith, love, and purposeful living. Build on the lessons learned from the previous days to set new intentions for next week.

In light of NaNa's profound insight, how do you perceive your journey thus far?

In light of NaNa's profound insight, how do you perceive your journey thus far?

Do you feel a sense of fulfillment or conviction when reflecting on your actions, words, love, and prayers offered?

The 2nd Pearl

Our frustrations often cause us to think that what "could've been" is better than "what IS." We shift our focus into a world of fantasy & mirage. We fail to see the artistry of GOD's work through the victory of overcoming our struggles - the years gone by were not ours to begin with - but a true gift from GOD; how you live them is your gift to HIM - we MUST take ownership for our faults while trying to "pin-point" those of others...the "blame-game" is the crucial ingredient for most failed relation-ships. Marriages/or relationships are never "perfect" or ideal. Still, they ARE complete...the "perfection" comes with each member's "investment" of love, time, prayer, communication, commitment, intimacies, compromise, faith, loyalty, forgiveness, & understanding. The safe opens with 365 to the right, 24 to the left, and 7 to the right: open to enjoy the tears/laughter & memories...

BE BLESSED & A BLESSING. LOVE ALL OF MY FB FRIENDS & SPECIAL LOVE TO ALL OF MY FAMILY ON THIS DAY

Embracing the Artistry of God's Work in Our Lives

As we gather at the start of this new week, let us turn our hearts and minds toward a profound truth that often eludes us amid life's challenges and frustrations. This truth reminds us of the beauty of

God's handiwork, the significance of our choices, and the power of love in our relationships.

In the hustle and bustle of our daily lives, it is easy to fall into the trap of dwelling on what "could've been" rather than embracing "what IS." Frustrations, disappointments, and unfulfilled dreams can lead us to create a world of fantasy and mirage in our minds, where we imagine alternate paths and different outcomes. Yet, in doing so, we often fail to see the artistry of God's work unfolding before us. The years gone by were never truly ours; they were a gift from God, a precious tapestry woven by the hands of the Divine. Our gift back to Him is how we live these years, how we navigate the ups and downs, the joys and sorrows.

In our journey through life, we must take ownership of our faults and shortcomings. The "blame game" is a corrosive force in many failed relationships, whether in marriages, friendships, or family dynamics. The poison erodes trust and understanding, leaving a trail of broken hearts and shattered connections.

Marriages and relationships are never perfect, nor are they meant to be. However, they are complete in their imperfections. True perfection emerges through investing in love, time, prayer, communication, commitment, intimacies, compromise, faith, loyalty, forgiveness, and understanding.

Imagine a safe with a combination lock that opens to reveal lifetime treasures. The code to unlock this safe is 365 to the right, 24 to the left, and 7 to the right. It symbolizes the daily commitment and constant availability required to enjoy the tears and laughter, the joys and sorrows, and the memories that make up the fabric of our lives.

Each day, as we turn the dial of time, we can invest in our relationships, nurture the bonds that connect us, and express our love meaningfully. In these moments of investment, we discover the true beauty of life and the depth of our connections.

As we start this new week, let us carry with us the wisdom of embracing the artistry of God's work in our lives. Let us release the burden of dwelling on what could have been and instead focus on what is. Let us take ownership of our actions, mend broken relationships, and invest in the love that can transform our lives.

May we be blessed and be a blessing to others. Let us love all those around us, whether they are our friends on social media or our cherished family members. Let us commit to living each day with intention, purpose, and the knowledge that God's grace and love surround us constantly.

In unity and love,

NaNa

By incorporating these daily activities into your life, you can embrace the artistry of God's work, strengthen your relationships, and live each day with purpose and intention. May you be blessed as you invest in love, understanding, and faith, which will enrich your life and the lives of those around you.

Day 1: Count Your Blessings: Start each day by counting your blessings. Reflect on the gifts and experiences God has bestowed upon you. Thank Him for the years past and the opportunities ahead.

Day 2: Practice Ownership and Forgiveness: Commit to owning your actions and faults. Reflect on any relationships that may have been strained by the "blame game." Reach out to someone you may have wronged and offer a heartfelt apology. Forgive those who have hurt you, freeing yourself from resentment.

Day 3: Invest in Your Relationships: Identify a relationship that needs nurturing. Whether it's a spouse, a family member, or a friend, reach out and invest time in meaningful communication. Share your thoughts, feelings, and aspirations, and listen openly.

Day 4: Embrace Imperfections: Remember that perfection is not the goal in your relationships. Embrace the imperfections and quirks that make each person unique. Celebrate the authenticity and beauty of accepting one another as we are.

Day 5: Show Unconditional Love: Make it a point to express unconditional love today. Whether through a kind word, a loving gesture, or a simple act of service, let love guide your interactions with others. Reflect on God's unconditional love for you and strive to emulate it.

Day 6: Reflect on Memories: Reflect on the memories you've created throughout your life's journey. Open the safe of your heart and revisit the tears, laughter, joys, and sorrows. Share stories and experiences with loved ones, keeping those memories alive.

Day 7: Commit to Daily Investment: As the week concludes, commit to daily investment in your relationships and faith. Set aside time daily for prayer, reflection, and connection with God. Dedicate yourself to nurturing the love, trust, and understanding in your relationships.

How do you perceive the balance between acknowledging frustrations and disappointments and recognizing the blessings and victories God has bestowed upon you?

How can you shift your focus from dwelling on 'what could've been' to embracing 'what is' and honoring God's artistry?

The 3rd Pearl

My other personality is "caged." Please don't "feed" the Tiger or let her out! She doesn't have her wings yet.

LOVE TO ALL MY FAMILY & FRIENDS

2 Timothy 1:7 (NIV): For the Spirit God gave us does not make us timid, but gives us power, love, and self-discipline.

This scripture reminds us that we have been given the Spirit of God, which empowers us to exercise self-discipline and control our actions and emotions, including the aspects of our personalities that may need restraint.

Ephesians 4:22-24 (NIV): "You were taught, about your former way of life, to put off your old self, which is being corrupted by its deceitful desires; to be made new in the attitude of your minds; and to put on the new self, created to be like God in true righteousness and holiness."

This passage encourages us to abandon our old ways and allow God to transform us into new creations. It emphasizes the importance of embracing a new self that aligns with God's righteousness and holiness and letting go of the aspects of our personalities that do not reflect His character.

Embracing Transformation:

As we gather at the beginning of this new week, let us delve into a profound NaNa Pearl that speaks to our dual nature: "My other personality is 'caged.' Please don't 'feed' the Tiger or let HER out!!! She doesn't have her wings yet." This striking metaphor reflects the inner struggle we all face, the tension between our old selves and the transformative power of God's Spirit.

Let us venture on an expedition to unlock the spiritual depth of these verses and understand how they resonate with the scriptures from 2 Timothy 1:7 and Ephesians 4:22-24.

Unlocking the Cage: The caged personality metaphor represents the aspects of ourselves that need restraint and transformation. We all have moments when our inner 'Tiger' of negative emotions, destructive habits, or sinful tendencies threatens to escape its confines. This 'Tiger' may manifest as anger, jealousy, pride, or any other sinful inclination.

"Please don't 'feed' the Tiger or let HER out!!!" This plea reminds us of the importance of self-control and self-discipline. When we feed our negative tendencies, we strengthen them and allow them to take control. Instead, we must rely on the Spirit of God to help us resist these temptations and keep our inner 'Tiger' at bay.

"She doesn't have her wings yet." This part of the Pearl reminds us that our old, sinful self is incompatible with the new creation God is shaping us to be, just as a caged bird that once flew freely and was wounded because of its flight path in the wrong direction and not at the proper altitude. It was injured by either hunters, turbulence, or crashing into obstacles because the elements blurred its sight. It is now in a cage, healing and being repaired from its injuries, and needs to undergo a process of transformation before it can spread its wings and fly again at the correct heights in the right direction; we, too, must undergo a spiritual transformation and the process of renewal to become more Christ-like.

Understanding the Scriptures:

2 Timothy 1:7 (NIV): "For the Spirit God gave us does not make us timid, but gives us power, love, and self-discipline." This scripture reminds us that through the Holy Spirit, God has equipped us with the power to overcome our sinful tendencies and exercise self-discipline. When we rely on His Spirit, we can resist the urge to 'feed the Tiger' within us and live with love, self-discipline, and a sound mind.

Ephesians 4:22-24 (NIV): "You were taught, about your former way of life, to put off your old self, which is being corrupted by its deceitful desires; to be made new in the attitude of your minds; and to put on the new self, created to be like God in true righteousness and holiness." This passage emphasizes the importance of shedding our old, sinful selves and embracing the transformative work of God's Spirit. It calls us to put on the new self, characterized by righteousness and holiness, just as a caged bird spreads its wings after transforming.

Embracing Transformation:

As we apply these teachings to our lives, we are called to unlock the cage of our old selves through the power of God's Spirit. We must exercise self-discipline, resisting the urge to feed our sinful tendencies, and instead, allow God to transform us into new creations.

In this new week, let us commit to relying on the Spirit of God, who empowers us to overcome our 'Tiger' and put on the new self, reflecting God's righteousness and holiness. As we do so, we will soar on the wings of His grace, leaving behind the old and embracing the transformative journey that leads to a closer likeness to Christ.

May this week be a week of growth, transformation, and victory over our old selves as we unlock the cage and soar with God.

In His grace and love,

NaNa

By incorporating these daily activities into your life, you can actively unlock the cage of your old self and embrace God's Spirit's transformative work. May each day bring you closer to living out the lessons of the scriptures, and may you experience the freedom and victory that come with embracing transformation in Christ.

Day 1: Reflect on Your 'Tiger': Begin your day by reflecting on the aspects of your old self you wish to transform. Identify the 'Tiger' within you - the negative emotions, habits, or sinful tendencies that need restraint. Write them down, acknowledging their presence.

Day 2: Seek God's Spirit: Incorporate a moment of prayer and meditation into your day. Ask for the guidance and strength of the Holy Spirit to help you resist feeding the 'Tiger' within. Pray for the power, love, and self-discipline described in 2 Timothy 1:7.

Day 3: Practice Self-Discipline: Today, practice self-discipline in an area where the 'Tiger' tends to emerge. It might be your reactions to others, spending habits, or time use. Take conscious steps to resist feeding the negative tendencies.

Day 4: Renew Your Mind: Reflect on Ephesians 4:22-24 and focus on renewing your mind. Identify any thought patterns that support your old self and replace them with thoughts that align with God's righteousness and holiness.

Day 5: Forgive and Release: Forgive yourself and others for past mistakes and offenses. Holding onto grudges and resentments can keep the 'Tiger' alive within you. Let go of these burdens and experience the freedom that comes with forgiveness.

Day 6: Connect with a Mentor or Accountability Partner: Reach out to a trusted friend, mentor, or accountability partner. Share your journey of transformation with them and seek their support. Having someone to walk alongside you can provide encouragement and accountability.

Day 7: Embrace Your New Self: At the end of the week, celebrate your progress. Embrace your emerging new self, characterized by God's righteousness and holiness. Rejoice in the transformation taking place within you.

About the 'caged tiger,' how do you perceive the aspects of your personality that you feel are 'caged' or restrained?

{34}

In what ways do you sense God calling you to nurture and cultivate these aspects while aligning them with His will and purpose for your life?

The 4th Pearl

The "birthing" process is painful—make the pain worthwhile by giving birth to Love, Peace, Forgiveness, Humility, Faithfulness, Kindness, Long-suffering, Patience, Prayer, and charity. Your "labor" will not be in vain. Gift Him this season to everyone you love and meet.

The Birthing of Virtues:

Making Pain Worthwhile

As we embark on the start of this new week, let us delve into the profound pearl of wisdom that encapsulates the essence of transformation and the beauty that emerges from the birthing process: "The 'birthing' process is painful - make the pain worthwhile: give birth to Love; Peace; Forgiveness; Humility; Faithfulness; Kindness; Longsuffering; Patience; Prayer; & Charity - Your 'labor' will not be in vain ... Gift Him this season to everyone you love & meet."

This message reminds us that life's journey can be likened to a birthing process. Just as childbirth is often accompanied by pain and discomfort, our transformation and growth can involve moments of struggle and difficulty. However, the key lies in making the pain worthwhile by giving birth to virtues that reflect the character of Christ.

Metaphysical Interpretation:

In a metaphysical sense, the 'birthing' process represents our life challenges and trials. These challenges can be likened to labor pains, discomfort, and struggle that test our character and faith. However, just as a mother's pain in childbirth is rewarded with the precious gift of new life, our struggles can lead to the birth of virtues within us.

Interpreted Spiritual Meaning:

From a spiritual perspective, this message calls us to embrace transformation and growth. It encourages us to cultivate and give birth to virtues such as Love, Peace, Forgiveness, Humility, Faithfulness, Kindness, Longsuffering, Patience, Prayer, and Charity. These virtues are gifts we offer to others and offerings to God, demonstrating our commitment to living in alignment with His will.

A verse that beautifully resonates with the message of giving birth to virtues despite the pain is found in **Romans 5:3-4 (NIV):** "Not only so, but we also glory in our sufferings because we know that suffering produces perseverance; perseverance, character; and character, hope."

This scripture emphasizes that even while suffering and pain are present, a transformative process is at work. Suffering can produce perseverance, which can lead to the development of character, which ultimately fosters hope.

Embrace the Virtuous 'Labor':

As we navigate this new week and life's journey, let us remember that our challenges are part of our character's 'birthing' process. Embrace the pain and discomfort as opportunities to give birth to Love, Peace, Forgiveness, Humility, Faithfulness, Kindness, Longsuffering, Patience, Prayer, and Charity.

May your 'labor' be a testament to your commitment to living a life that reflects Christ's virtues. As we approach this season, let us gift these virtues to everyone we love and meet, spreading the Love, hope, and grace that flow from our transformed hearts. May your 'labor' not be in vain, but instead, may it bring forth the beauty of Christ's character in your life and bless those around you.

In His Love and grace,

NaNa

By incorporating these daily activities into your life, you can actively give birth to the virtues of Love, Peace, Forgiveness, Humility, Faithfulness, Kindness, Patience, and Prayer. As you navigate life's challenges and struggles, may you find that the pain of transformation is worthwhile, and may these virtues enrich your spiritual journey and bless those around you.

Day 1: Cultivate Love: Begin your week by consciously practicing Love. Choose to love even when it's complicated. Show kindness and compassion to someone who may be challenging to love. In doing so, you give birth to the virtue of Love in your actions.

Day 2: Pursue Peace: On this day, actively seek Peace in your interactions. When faced with conflict or tension, strive to be a peacemaker. Let go of resentments and grudges, and give birth to the virtue of Peace by promoting harmony and reconciliation.

Day 3: Extend Forgiveness: Reflect on your heart's lingering grudges or unforgiveness. Then, decide to forgive someone who may have hurt you. By doing so, you nurture the virtue of forgiveness and release the burden of bitterness.

Day 4: Embrace Humility: Practice humility by placing the needs and interests of others above your own. Seek opportunities to serve and uplift those around you without seeking recognition. Humility is the birthplace of many virtues.

Day 5: Remain Faithful: Choose to remain faithful in moments of doubt or uncertainty. Trust in God's plan and promises. Your steadfast faith will give birth to the virtue of Faithfulness and inspire others to trust in God.

Day 6: Show Kindness: Intentionally perform acts of kindness throughout your day. Extend a helping hand, offer encouraging words, or perform random acts of kindness to strangers. Kindness is a virtue that multiplies as it is shared.

Day 7: Practice Patience and Prayer: As the week comes to a close, practice the virtues of Patience and Prayer. When faced with delays or frustrations, exercise patience. Use this time to deepen your connection with God through prayer. Seek His guidance, strength, and wisdom in all you do.

How can you turn life's challenges into opportunities to birth virtues like Love, Peace, and forgiveness, making your efforts worthwhile and a gift to others?

My Cup Runneth Over

The 5th Pearl

All wealth is not in the bank - and for that, I am thankful - plus, I am also VERY wealthy: love, the respect of friends and family and most of all, GOD's favor. He has opened the floodgates of Heaven for me. So let it Rain.

Counting Blessings Beyond Wealth

As we gather to commence another week, let us reflect upon the profound message conveyed by the Scriptures in Proverbs 22:1, "A good name is more desirable than great riches; to be esteemed is better than silver or gold." This verse encapsulates the timeless truth that true wealth extends beyond material possessions, encompassing the value of a sterling reputation, the love and respect of friends and family, and the immeasurable favor of our Heavenly Father. It reminds us that spiritual riches far surpass worldly wealth.

We are reminded that we are incredibly wealthy. The declaration, "I am also VERY wealthy," resonates deeply within us, urging us to pause and reflect on the abundant blessings that grace our lives. Our wealth is not measured by the dollars in our bank accounts but by the love and respect bestowed upon us by cherished friends and family. It is found in the relationships we nurture, the shared laughter, and the comforting embrace during times of sorrow.

Most profoundly, we are reminded of the boundless wealth that emanates from God's favor. The author's unwavering faith resonates in saying, "He has opened the floodgates of Heaven for me." This is a beautiful testament to the divine blessings that cascade into our lives each day. When we walk in faith, trusting in the Lord, our lives are inundated with His grace, mercy, and love.

The imagery of God opening the floodgates of Heaven is both powerful and poignant. It signifies the limitless abundance God is ready to pour into our lives when we open our hearts to Him. Just as rain quenches the thirst of a parched and barren land, God's favor satisfies the yearning of our souls. Like refreshing raindrops, his blessings descend upon us without measure, nourishing our spirits and filling us with hope.

Let us take a moment to ponder the myriad ways in which God's favor has enriched our lives. Consider the instances when He guided us through life's storms, provided for our needs, and enveloped us in His boundless love. Every act of kindness, every moment of serenity, and every answered prayer is a testament to His infinite favor.

As we go forth in our day, let us carry this profound pearl of wisdom message in our hearts. Let us remember that genuine wealth resides in the love and respect we share with our fellow human beings and in the unwavering favor of our Heavenly Father. Let us rejoice in the assurance that, in His divine timing and manner, God will open the floodgates of Heaven for each one of us.

Therefore, dear brothers and sisters, let it rain. Let God's blessings shower upon us as we continue our faith journey. Let us be grateful for the wealth that genuinely matters—the wealth of love, respect, and God's favor. May we live each day in the radiance of this truth, sharing our abundance with others and radiating the joy of hearts overflowing with gratitude.

In His grace.

NaNa

By incorporating these daily activities into your life, you can culti-vate a deeper appreciation for the spiritual wealth highlighted in "NaNa's Pearls" and the lessons from Proverbs 22:1, Matthew 6:19-21, and Psalm 84:11. These practices will not only enrich your own life but also help you become a beacon of love, respect, and faith to those around you.

Day 1: Reflect on Your Spiritual Wealth: Take a few moments each morning to reflect on the non-material blessings in your life. Consider your reputation, the love and respect of your family and friends, and the favor of God. Express gratitude for these riches in your prayers.

Day 2: Cultivate Good Relationships: Make an intentional effort to strengthen your relationships. Reach out to a family member or friend you haven't connected with. Share love and respect by offering words of encouragement and affirmation.

Day 3: Give to Those in Need: In alignment with Matthew 6:19-21, focus on storing treasures in Heaven by giving to those less fortu-nate. Donate to a charitable cause, volunteer your time, or perform a random act of kindness for someone in need.

Day 4: Practice Contentment: Throughout the day, remember that material possessions don't measure true wealth. When you desire more, pause and reflect on your spiritual riches, especially God's favor; let this contentment guide your actions and thoughts.

Day 5: Share Words of Encouragement: Use your words to build up others. Send a heartfelt message or note of encouragement to a friend or family member. Let them know how much you appreci-ate and respect them.

Day 6: Seek God's Favor Through Prayer: Devote time to pray and seek God's favor. Pray for guidance, wisdom, and the strength to walk in righteousness. Express your gratitude for the favor God has already bestowed upon you.

Day 7: Reflect on Your Journey: As the week concludes, journal or meditate on the lessons learned. Reflect on the richness of your life beyond material possessions and commit to continuing these daily practices of gratitude, love, and faith in God's favor.

In recognizing wealth beyond material possessions, including love, respect, and God's favor in your life, how do you intend to steward and nurture these blessings to honor God and enrich the lives of those around you?

{50}

The 6th Pearl

You can't spend your life in the graveyard of guilt dealing with the corpses of the past. Know when things are dead and when to release and bury them. If you continue to work with the dry bones of dead issues, you, too, will begin to decay. No amount of work will resurrect a corpse. Sign the death certificate and bury the past.

Resurrecting Your Life: Burying the Past. Start Your Week with Renewed Hope

As we gather at the beginning of this new week, let us reflect on a powerful pearl of wisdom: "You can't spend your life in the graveyard of guilt dealing with the corpses of the past. Know when things are dead and when to release and bury them. If you continue to work with the dry bones of dead issues, you, too, will begin to decay. No amount of work will resurrect a corpse. Sign the death certificate and bury the past." This profound wisdom reminds us of the importance of recognizing when certain aspects of our lives are past their expiration date and must be laid to rest. Today, we will explore three Bible verses that shed light on this wisdom's literal, spiritual, and metaphysical meanings.

Ezekiel 37:1-4 - The Vision of Dry Bones:

"The hand of the Lord was on me, and he brought me out by the Spirit of the Lord and set me in the middle of a valley full of bones. He led me back and forth among them, and I saw a great many bones on the floor of the valley that were very dry. He asked me, 'Son of man, can these bones live?' I said, 'Sovereign Lord, you alone know.'"

Literal Meaning: In this vision, Ezekiel sees a valley filled with dry bones, symbolizing God's people's spiritual deadness and hopelessness. These dry bones represent areas of our lives or situations that have become lifeless, just like the past issues we hold onto.

Spiritual Meaning: Just as God breathed life into these dry bones and brought them back to life, He can breathe new life into our lives. It's essential to recognize when dealing with dead issues and trust that God can resurrect and rejuvenate us spiritually.

Metaphysical Meaning: Dry bones also symbolize the emotional and psychological baggage we carry from the past. Continuing to work with these "dry bones" keeps us trapped in the past and hinders our growth and transformation.

Philippians 3:13-14 - Forgetting What Lies Behind:

"Brothers and sisters, I do not consider myself yet to have taken hold of it. But one thing I do: Forgetting what is behind and straining toward what is ahead, I press on toward the goal to win the prize for which God has called me heavenward in Christ Jesus."

Literal Meaning: The Apostle Paul urges us to forget what lies behind us, acknowledge that we have not yet attained perfection, and continue pursuing spiritual growth.

Spiritual Meaning: Just as Paul focuses on pressing forward in his spiritual journey, we must strive for progress rather than dwelling on past failures or sins.

Metaphysical Meaning: Dwelling on the past can hinder our present and future. We must release the past to fully embrace God's blessings for us today.

Colossians 3:13 - Bearing with One Another:
"Bear with each other and forgive one another if any of you has a grievance against someone. Forgive as the Lord forgave you."

Literal Meaning: This verse reminds us to bear with one another and forgive those who wronged us.

Spiritual Meaning: Forgiveness is crucial to releasing the past. Holding onto grudges or past hurts can hinder our spiritual growth and walk with Christ.

Metaphysical Meaning: By letting go of bitterness and resentment, we free ourselves from emotional and psychological burdens, allowing us to live more abundantly in the present.

As we embark on this week, let us remember that God offers us the opportunity to bury the past, release the dead issues, and move forward in His grace and love.

In His Grace. Amen.

NaNa

Day 1: Meditate on Ezekiel 37:1-4. Reflect on any "dry bones" in your life that need resurrection. Pray for God's renewal.

Day 2: Read and contemplate Philippians 3:13-14. Identify any past issues holding you back and list steps to move forward.

Day 3: Study Colossians 3:13. Reach out to someone you need to forgive or seek forgiveness from.

Day 4: Spend the day in prayer and ask God to reveal any lingering guilt or regrets from your past. Surrender them to Him.

Day 5: Create a "Release List" of past issues you must let go of. Symbolically bury it as a declaration of moving forward.

Day 6: Seek counsel or support from a trusted friend or mentor to help you navigate the process of burying the past.

Day 7: Bible study on renewal and resurrection. Share your experiences and insights with fellow believers.

In your spiritual growth and healing journey, how do you discern when to release and bury the burdens of guilt and past mistakes, trusting God's forgiveness and grace to guide you toward renewal and restoration?

NAOMI K. PETTIFORD

The 7th Pearl

History has proven it's easier to take the "Africa" out of a people than the "bullcrap" they have nurtured themselves on. For that, you need a "special laxative" with the ingredients of Pride, Integrity, & Self-worth," which are not sold at your local supermarkets or 'fast-food' joints. It's not even on the shelves at your local Wal-Mart pharmacies.

Nurturing Your Inner Worth: A Spiritual Journey

Dear brothers and sisters in Christ, as we embark on this new week, let us reflect on the profound wisdom of this powerful statement. Let us turn to the Word of God to understand this powerful statement's spiritual and metaphysical implications. Proverbs 16:18 reminds us, "Pride goes before destruction and a haughty spirit before a fall." This verse teaches us that excessive pride can lead to our downfall, and we must remain humble in the eyes of the Lord.

Furthermore, 1 Corinthians 6:19-20 states, "Or do you not know that your body is a temple of the Holy Spirit within you, whom you have from God? You are not your own, for you were bought with a price. So glorify God in your body." These verses emphasize the importance of integrity and self-worth. Our bodies are temples of the Holy Spirit, and we must honor God through our actions and choices.

Finally, Psalm 139:14 reminds us of our intrinsic value in God's eyes: "I praise you, for I am fearfully and wonderfully made. Wonderful are your works; my soul knows them very well." This verse underscores the importance of recognizing our self-worth as individuals uniquely created by God.

The lessons we can draw from these verses are as relevant today in 2024 as ever. In a world filled with distractions, temptations, and pressures to conform, we must hold fast to our Christian identity and values. The special laxative of Pride, Integrity, and Self-worth allows us to cleanse ourselves from the falsehoods and negative influences that surround us.

Consider this: In today's world, the constant comparison on social media can erode our self-worth, making us feel inadequate. However, by anchoring our self-worth in God's love and recognizing that we are fearfully and wonderfully made, we can resist the pull of insecurity and embrace our unique identity.

May this week be a time of inner transformation as we seek to cleanse ourselves with the special laxative of Pride, Integrity, and Self-worth, drawing closer to God and living out our faith with authenticity and grace.

In His Grace. Amen.

NaNa

Day 1: Reflect on Proverbs 16:18 and pray for humility.

Day 2: Meditate on 1 Corinthians 6:19-20 and make righteous choices.

Day 3: Repeat Psalm 139:14 as a daily mantra, reminding yourself of your worth.

Day 4: Identify one area where pride has hindered your growth and work on letting it go.

Day 5: Review your thoughts on integrity and how you can uphold it in your daily interactions.

Day 6: Encourage a friend or family member by reminding them of their worth in God's eyes.

Day 7: On this day of our spiritual journey, let's focus on spreading kindness in our workplaces, schools, or neighborhoods, applying the principles of Pride, Integrity, and Self-worth. Your assignment is to perform at least three acts of kindness throughout the day, reflecting God's love in our daily lives. Remember Galatians 6:9: "Let us not grow weary of doing good." By spreading kindness, we uplift others and reflect God's presence in our midst, reminding us that our faith extends beyond church walls.

How has your cultural or societal upbringing influenced the beliefs and values you hold dear? Reflect on any detrimental "bullcrap" narratives or mindsets that you may have internalized over time and consider how they have hindered your personal growth and spiritual development.

How can you cultivate and integrate the "special laxatives" of Pride, Integrity, and Self-worth into your life despite their scarcity in mainstream sources? Explore how prioritizing these qualities can lead to a more profound sense of authenticity, resilience, and alignment with God's purpose for your life.

The 8th Pearl

Do you mean to tell me that we have "championed" Jim Crow legalism, the Willie Lynch mentality, the Back-of-the-Bus era, the KKK terminators, the "tamper-with-the-vote majority, the seize-your-house bank breakers, the "back-to-Africa" tourist trade, the "you're over-educated, over-qualified" job re-routers. And put a Black Man in the White House; not one term, but two. To be "challenged" with a "cliff" that we never knew existed? If we fall over it, so be it? As far as I'm concerned, the only way "up" is "down" but not on my "luck" —on my knees & face (if need be) before MY GOD who IS my Jehovah Jireh. HE WILL PROVIDE AND NEVER NEEDS A "BAIL-OUT" BECAUSE HE NEVER FAILS. TRY HIM TODAY. YOU'LL BE GLAD YOU DID

Rising Above the Challenges: Trusting in Jehovah Jireh

As we embark on a new week, let us gather in the presence of the Lord to meditate on the profound pearl of wisdom, and in these words, we are reminded of the challenges and obstacles that have marked the journey of a people and, indeed, all humanity. Historically and in our modern times, we have faced trials and tribulations. Yet, in the face of adversity, we find a glimmer of hope and an unshakable truth in the Scriptures.

Let us turn our hearts to the book of Genesis, chapter 22, verse 14, which reads, "So Abraham called that place The Lord Will Provide. And to this day, it is said, 'On the mountain of the Lord it will be provided." This literal and spiritual verse teaches us that God remains our provider even in the most challenging circumstances. Just as He provided a ram for Abraham in his time of need, He is always there to supply our material or spiritual needs. It is easy to feel overwhelmed by today's uncertainties, economic struggles, and societal pressures. However, the lesson from Genesis 22:14 is as relevant now as it was in the past. We must remember that God is our Jehovah Jireh, our provider, and we can trust Him to meet our needs. As we face economic challenges, political unrest, and personal hardships in 2024, we can take comfort in knowing that God is our unwavering source of strength. In our daily lives, we can witness God's provision in various ways. Take a moment to observe the flowers in a garden. They do not toil or spin, yet God clothes them in splendor (Matthew 6:28-29). Similarly, we can see His provision in the kindness of a stranger, a job opportunity when we least expect it, or the love and support of our friends and family. God's provision is not always material wealth but often comes from His grace and mercy.

In conclusion, as we face the challenges of 2024, let us remember the promise in Genesis 22:14. God is our provider, our Jehovah Jireh, and He will never fail us. Let us trust in Him, seek His face in prayer, and carry His love and provision into our daily lives, shining as beacons of hope.

In His Grace. Amen

NaNa

By incorporating these daily activities into your life, you can embark on a transformative journey in 2024, deepening your faith, spreading love, and living a purposeful life guided by the wisdom and insights from our shared journey. May each day bring you closer to the path of love, grace, and fulfillment God has prepared for you.

Day 1: Start each day with a prayer of gratitude for God's provision in your life, big and small.

Day 2: Reflect on your community's needs and find a way to contribute or volunteer to help those less fortunate.

Day 3: Take time to read and meditate on Psalm 23, which reminds us that the Lord is our shepherd and provides for all our needs.

Day 4: Reach out to someone who may be going through a tough time and offer them words of encouragement and support.

Day 5: Practice contentment by focusing on your blessings rather than what you lack.

Day 6: Set aside some of your income to give to a charitable cause or support a missionary organization.

Day 7: Gather with your church community to share testimonies of God's provision and encourage one another in faith.

How does your faith in God's provision and sovereignty influence your perspective on facing challenges and adversity, particularly in the context of societal injustices and historical struggles?

Reflecting on the resilience and faithfulness demonstrated in NaNa's Pearl, how do you see God's hand at work in your life journey, especially in times of uncertainty or when encountering seemingly insurmountable obstacles?

The 9th Pearl

Change will always come, whether we like it or not, especially when GOD takes us to a new level in HIS purpose. Just KNOW: we don't "choose" our change, but we DO have to choose our "God."

Embracing Change with Faith

Dear beloved, as we embark on this new week, let us meditate upon the wisdom encapsulated in the NaNa's Pearl: "Change will always come whether we like it or not, especially when GOD is taking us to a new level in HIS purpose. Just KNOW: we don't 'choose' our change, but we DO have to choose our 'God.'"

Proverbs 3:5-6 (NIV): "Trust in the Lord with all your heart and lean not on your understanding; in all your ways submit to him, and he will make your paths straight." This scripture reminds us that we may not always understand the changes that come our way, but we must trust in the Lord with all our hearts and acknowledge His sovereignty over our lives. By submitting to His will, we allow Him to guide our paths, even when those paths lead us through uncertain times.

In 2024, we are constantly faced with unexpected challenges and transformations. This scripture's message is as relevant today as it was in ancient times. We must learn to trust God's plan, even when change is uncomfortable or unwelcome. We can find peace and purpose amid change by surrendering our understanding and seeking God's guidance.

Imagine a young adult starting a new job in a different city, leaving behind the familiar comforts of home. They may initially struggle with the change, feeling overwhelmed by the unknown. However, by trusting in God's plan and seeking His guidance through prayer and faith, they can confidently navigate this transition and discover new opportunities and blessings.

In His Grace. Amen.

NaNa

May this week be a journey of faith and trust in God's unchanging love, even in constant change. Remember, we may not choose our change, but we can choose our God.

Day 1: Spend prayer, surrendering your plans and uncertainties to God and asking for His guidance in the changes you face.

Day 2: Take a nature walk and reflect on the beauty of God's creation. Use this time to meditate on His sovereignty over the changes in your life.

Day 3: Reach out to a friend or family member going through a difficult change, offering your support and prayers.

Day 4: Read a book or watch a sermon that inspires you to trust God's plan in times of change.

Day 5: Listen to worship music that reminds you of God's faithfulness and ability to guide you through any change.

Day 6: Volunteer or act kindly for someone in need, reflecting God's love and grace in your actions.

Day 7: Join a small group or Bible study to deepen your faith and connect with others who can encourage and support you during life's changes.

How do you perceive the changes in your life, especially when God is leading you to a new level in His purpose? Reflect on how you have navigated change in the past and are currently embracing it in your faith journey.

How intentional are you in aligning your decisions and actions with God's will and purpose for your life during change? Consider the areas where you may need to surrender control and trust in God's guidance, acknowledging that He orchestrates change for our ultimate good.

As you contemplate the inevitability of change and the necessity of choosing God in every aspect of your life, how are you actively cultivating a deeper relationship with Him? Explore ways to deepen your faith and reliance on God amidst life's uncertainties, recognizing that He alone holds the keys to true transformation and fulfillment.

The 10th Pearl

Our enemies are not giants, but our minds' delusions make them gigantic. Declare victory over yourself against every enemy attack, including the devil, the world system, and yourself.

Declaring Victory Over Spiritual Giants

1 John 4:4 (NIV): You, dear children, are from God and have overcome them because the one who is in you is greater than the one who is in the world.

This scripture reassures us of our identity as children of God and reminds us of the power that resides within us through the Holy Spirit. It signifies that no matter our challenges or adversaries, God's presence within us is more significant, and we can overcome through Him.

The essence of this Pearl Of Wisdom lies in recognizing the true nature of our spiritual battles. Often, we perceive our obstacles and adversaries as insurmountable giants, looming large and intimidating. However, the truth is that these enemies are less formidable than they seem. The illusions created by our minds, fueled by fear and doubt, magnify their stature. By declaring victory over ourselves, we acknowledge the authority and power of God within us, which enables us to conquer every enemy attack, whether it be from the devil, the world system, or our sinful nature.

In the complexities of modern-day life in 2024, we encounter various challenges that can easily overwhelm us. From societal pressures to personal struggles, it's easy to perceive these obstacles as formidable giants threatening to defeat us. However, the lesson from this Pearl Of Wisdom and 1 John 4:4 is timeless and relevant. We are reminded that our true strength lies not in our abilities but in the power of God dwelling within us. By acknowledging this truth and declaring victory over ourselves, we can face any challenge with confidence and assurance, knowing that we are more than conquerors through Christ.

Consider a young professional navigating the competitive landscape of their industry. They may encounter numerous setbacks and obstacles that appear daunting and impossible. Yet, by embracing the truth of 1 John 4:4 and declaring victory over themselves, they can approach their challenges with courage and faith, trusting in God's strength to guide them to success.

Much Love,

NaNa

May this week be a testament to our victory in Christ as we declare triumph over every spiritual giant that seeks to intimidate and defeat us.

Day 1: Begin the week with a guided meditation or prayer, declaring victory over yourself and surrendering your fears and doubts to God.

Day 2: Engage in physical exercise, such as a brisk walk or yoga, to invigorate your body and mind, reinforcing the truth of your strength in God.

Day 3: Reach out to a friend or family member facing a difficult situation, offering encouragement and reminding them of their victory in Christ.

Day 4: Study and reflect on scriptures affirming God's victory in your life, strengthening your faith and resolve.

- Romans 8:37

- 1 Corinthians 15:57

- 2 Corinthians 2:14

- 1 John 5:4

- Ephesians 6:10

Day 5: Join a virtual Bible study or Christian fellowship group to connect with other believers and share testimonies of God's faithfulness in overcoming obstacles.

Day 6: Volunteer or engage in acts of service within your community, demonstrating the love and power of God to overcome adversity.

Day 7: Gather with fellow believers for worship and prayer, celebrating the victories God has brought forth in your lives and affirming your collective strength in Him.

Reflect on a time when you faced a challenge or obstacle that seemed impossible, either internally or externally. How did your perception of the challenge influence your response and actions?

My Cup Runneth Over

Considering NaNa's Pearl of Wisdom, consider how your mindset and beliefs contributed to viewing the challenge as larger than life. How can you declare victory over yourself and overcome similar challenges in the future, recognizing the enemy's true nature and relying on God's strength?

Explore instances where you've battled against spiritual or mental adversaries, such as doubts, fears, or negative thought patterns. How did these adversaries manifest, and what strategies did you employ to confront them?

Drawing from NaNa's Pearl of Wisdom, analyze how your perception of these adversaries influenced your ability to overcome them. How can you declare victory over yourself against every enemy attack moving forward, leveraging your faith and understanding of the true nature of spiritual warfare?

My Cup Runneth Over

{91}

The 11th Pearl

When pursuing your passion, developing your dreams, or manifesting your ministry while dealing with self-doubt, remember that no matter how many "no's" you get from man, just one "yes" from God is all you need. Be "the proof in your pudding."

Proverbs 3:5-6 underscores the importance of trusting in God's guidance and sovereignty. It encourages believers to abandon their limited understanding and wholeheartedly trust God's wisdom. By surrendering control to Him and submitting to His will in every aspect of life, we can witness His faithfulness in guiding our paths toward fulfillment and purpose.

2 Corinthians 1:20 echoes this sentiment, highlighting the divine assurance found in Christ. This verse reaffirms God's unwavering commitment to fulfilling His promises. It transcends mere words, speaking to God's affirmation's spiritual and metaphysical dimensions, surpassing human limitations and doubts.

The fundamental lesson is to trust God's steadfast faithfulness, not human validation. Amidst today's self-doubt and societal pressures, remembering that God's "Yes" outweighs any human "No" offers solace and resilience. By internalizing this truth, we cultivate perseverance and trust, essential virtues for navigating life's challenges.

In today's fast-paced and competitive world, individuals often face rejection and setbacks in various aspects of life, whether career aspirations, personal goals, or spiritual endeavors. This scripture is a timeless beacon of hope, reminding us to remain steadfast in our faith despite external discouragement. Whether in the workplace, social circles, or personal endeavors, trusting in God's "Yes" remains relevant, offering comfort and strength amidst uncertainty.

Consider a scenario where someone faces multiple job rejections despite their qualifications and efforts. Amid disappointment and self-doubt, they receive an unexpected job offer that aligns perfectly with their skills and passions. This is a tangible manifestation of God's "Yes" amidst the world's "Nos," reaffirming the principle illustrated in 2 Corinthians 1:20.

In His Grace. Amen.

NaNa

By incorporating these daily activities centered around the Pearl of Wisdom and scripture verse, Christians can cultivate a resilient faith that transcends earthly setbacks and doubts, finding assurance in God's unwavering "Yes" amidst life's challenges.

Day 1: Start your week by creating a digital vision board outlining your aspirations and dreams. Reflect on 2 Corinthians 1:20 as you visualize your goals, trusting God's ultimate affirmation.

Day 2: Engage in a physical exercise routine, whether a morning jog, yoga session, or gym workout. As you push your physical limits, meditate on God's strength in overcoming obstacles, drawing inspiration from His unwavering "Yes."

Day 3: Reach out to a friend or family member facing discouragement or self-doubt. Offer words of encouragement rooted in the truth of God's faithfulness, reminding them of His ultimate affirmation in their lives.

Day 4: Dedicate time for personal reflection and journaling. Write down instances where you've experienced God's faithfulness in the face of adversity, reinforcing your trust in His promises, as outlined in 2 Corinthians 1:20.

Day 5: Share an uplifting message or scripture on your social media platforms, spreading hope and encouragement to your online community. Let your words be a testament to God's unwavering "Yes" amid life's uncertainties.

Day 6: Volunteer or engage in a community service project, actively demonstrating God's love and faithfulness to those in need. As you serve others, embody the principle of being "the proof in your pudding," reflecting God's goodness through your actions.

Day 7: Attend a church service or virtual worship gathering. Reflect on the sermon's message, focusing on God's promises and His ultimate affirmation in your life. Share your reflections with fellow believers, fostering a community grounded in faith and encouragement.

Reflecting on your experiences thus far, describe a time when self-doubt threatened to hinder your pursuit of your passion, development of your dreams, or manifestation of your ministry. How did this self-doubt manifest, and what challenges did it present to your journey?

In the face of self-doubt, NaNa's Pearl of Wisdom reminds us that even amidst numerous "no's" from man, just one "yes" from God can be the ultimate affirmation and validation of our endeavors. How has your faith in God's approval and guidance influenced your response to self-doubt?

Can you recall a specific instance where God's affirmation was a beacon of hope and reassurance in your journey?

NaNa's Pearl encourages us to "be the proof in your pudding"—to trust our abilities, convictions, and God-given talents despite external skepticism or negativity. Reflecting on your journey, how have you embraced this principle in pursuing your passions, dreams, or ministry?

How have you demonstrated resilience, perseverance, and unwavering faith in self-doubt, ultimately becoming a living testament to your potential and God's faithfulness?

The 12th Pearl

There's no honor in our current administration of government - Man whose "hope" is in Man has NO hope and is "incarcerated" by his own ignorance and hatred.

Thomas Jefferson said: "When the people fear the government, there is tyranny. When the government fears the people, there is liberty."

In pursuing divine wisdom and spiritual enlightenment, we are often confronted with the stark realities of our earthly existence. Today, as we gather to commence this new week, let us reflect upon the profound words encapsulated within this Pearl Of Wisdom and echoed through the annals of history by the esteemed Thomas Jefferson: "When the people fear the government, there is tyranny. When the government fears the people, there is liberty."

These words, resonating with timeless truth, underscore the fundamental principle that a nation's governance should emanate from its populace's collective will and consciousness. When individuals relinquish their agency and entrust their hopes solely to human institutions, they inadvertently surrender their freedom to the whims of earthly powers. Yet, when governance is grounded in a healthy reverence for the people it serves, liberty flourishes, and the spirit of democracy thrives.

Turning to Scripture, we find resonance with this wisdom in Proverbs 29:25, which declares, "The fear of man lays a snare, but whoever trusts in the Lord is safe." This verse cautions against placing undue trust in human systems and offers a profound spiritual truth. When our trust is anchored in the Divine, we find proper security and liberation from worldly anxieties and uncertainties.

The relevance of these insights cannot be overstated as we navigate the complexities of our modern world. In an era marked by political strife, social unrest, and technological advancements, it is imperative that we, as Christians, remain vigilant in upholding the principles of justice, accountability, and compassion. Each day allows us to embody the timeless Wisdom Pearls and be inspired by the Scriptures.

Consider, for instance, the simple act of engaging in digital advocacy. By leveraging the power of social media and online platforms, we can amplify marginalized voices, hold elected officials accountable, and foster a culture of transparency and accountability in governance. Likewise, dedicating time to physical acts of service within our communities—such as volunteering at local shelters or participating in peaceful protests—becomes a tangible expression of our commitment to justice and freedom.

In our social interactions, let us emulate the humility and empathy exemplified by Jesus Christ, recognizing every individual's inherent dignity and worth. Through acts of kindness, active listening, and dialogue, we can cultivate a mutual respect and understanding of culture, transcending divisive rhetoric and fostering unity within our diverse society.

Moreover, as we engage in mental exercises such as prayer, meditation, and reflection, let us continually surrender our fears and anxieties to a higher power, trusting in divine providence to guide our paths. In doing so, we liberate ourselves from the shackles of fear and uncertainty, embracing a faith that transcends temporal limitations and empowers us to effect meaningful change in the world.

In pursuing spiritual growth and societal transformation, may we remain steadfast in our commitment to embodying the principles of liberty, justice, and compassion. Through our daily actions and interactions, let us be beacons of hope and agents of change in a world yearning for truth and liberation.

In His Grace. Amen.

NaNa

By incorporating these daily activities into your life, you can embark on a transformative journey in 2024, deepening your faith, spreading love, and living a purposeful life guided by the wisdom and insights from our shared journey. May each day bring you closer to the path of love, grace, and fulfillment God has prepared for you.

Day 1: Share an insightful article or social media post highlighting issues of justice and accountability in governance. Encourage constructive dialogue and awareness among your online community.

Day 2: Participate in a peaceful protest or community service activity to advocate for the rights and dignity of marginalized individuals or groups.

Day 3: Engage in a meaningful conversation with someone from different backgrounds or perspectives. Practice active listening and seek to understand their experiences and viewpoints with empathy and respect.

Day 4: Set aside time for prayer, meditation, or journaling. Reflect on your hopes, fears, and aspirations, surrendering them to a higher power and trusting in divine guidance.

Day 5: Take time to educate yourself on current political issues and the functioning of government institutions. Empower yourself with the knowledge to engage actively in civic discourse and advocacy.

Day 6: Perform a random act of kindness for a needy stranger or neighbor. Whether a small gesture or a significant offering, cultivate a spirit of generosity and compassion in your daily interactions.

Day 7: Attend a local town hall meeting or civic gathering. Voice your concerns, ask questions, and hold elected officials accountable for their actions and decisions. Your participation contributes to the people's collective voice and fosters a culture of transparency and accountability in governance.

In light of NaNa's Pearl of Wisdom, how does placing hope in human institutions or individuals align with your understanding of faith and spiritual principles? Reflect on how investing hope solely in human endeavors may lead to a sense of imprisonment by our own ignorance and biases, and consider how redirecting our hope towards God's sovereignty and guidance can bring true liberation and fulfillment in life.

The 13th Pearl

If a conversation were like a rich and black coffee, it would still not be pleasing to everyone's taste and stirred. ' It would not change; it would still be rich and black, nothing added (not action).

The Unchanging Richness of Conversation

- "Let your conversation be always full of grace, seasoned with salt, so that you may know how to answer everyone." - Colossians 4:6 (NIV)

- "A gentle answer turns away wrath, but a harsh word stirs up anger." - Proverbs 15:1 (NIV)

In the symbolic realm, the act of conversation mirrors the essence of coffee – rich and black, symbolizing depth and authenticity. Just as coffee maintains its richness irrespective of being stirred, our discussions should possess a similar unchanging richness. Colossians 4:6 urges us to season our words with grace, akin to adding flavor to coffee. This scripture underscores the importance of maintaining a gracious demeanor in our interactions, enriching them with kindness and understanding. Proverbs 15:1 highlights the power of gentle words in diffusing conflict, emphasizing the transformative potential of our speech.

Key Points and Life Lessons:

Authenticity in Communication: Like rich coffee, authentic conversations remain unchanged by external influences. Authenticity lies at the heart of genuine conversation. Like a rich cup of coffee, external influences keep authentic communication unaltered. This means expressing oneself sincerely, without pretense or the need for validation. Authentic conversations are characterized by transparency, vulnerability, and a willingness to engage with others meaningfully. When we embrace authenticity, we create space for deeper connections and genuine relationships to flourish.

Graceful Speech: Our words should be seasoned with grace, embodying kindness and understanding. Graceful speech is like seasoning our words with kindness, empathy, and understanding. Just as salt enhances food's flavor, grace enhances our communication's impact. It involves speaking with love and compassion, even in challenging situations. Graceful speech acknowledges the inherent worth of every individual and seeks to build others up rather than tear them down. By cultivating a habit of speaking graciously, we can foster trust, respect, and harmony in our interactions.

Conflict Resolution: Gentle responses can de-escalate tensions and foster reconciliation. Conflict is inevitable in human relationships, but how we respond can make all the difference. The proverbial wisdom in Proverbs 15:1 underscores the power of gentle words in diffusing tension and resolving disputes. Instead of responding with anger or hostility, gentle answers can disarm conflict and promote reconciliation. Conflict resolution requires humility, patience, and a commitment to seek understanding rather than asserting our perspectives. By choosing gentleness over aggression, we can transform conflict into an opportunity for growth and mutual respect.

In today's fast-paced digital age, conversations often lack depth and authenticity, becoming diluted by superficiality. Yet, the timeless wisdom of these scriptures reminds us of the enduring value of genuine communication. Whether online or in-person, our words can either uplift or diminish others. By embodying grace and gentleness in our speech, we can cultivate meaningful connections and promote harmony in an increasingly fragmented world.

Imagine a heated discussion on social media where differing opinions escalate into conflict. By applying Proverbs 15:1's principle of gentle responses, individuals can steer the conversation toward constructive dialogue, fostering understanding and empathy amidst diversity.

By embracing the unchanging richness of authentic conversation and seasoning our speech with grace and gentleness, we can foster deeper connections and promote harmony in our relationships. By intentionally practicing and applying biblical principles daily, we can cultivate a culture of empathy and understanding in our communities and embody the transformative power of Christ's love in our daily interactions.

One Love.

NaNa

My Cup Runneth Over

By incorporating these daily activities into your life, you can embark on a transformative journey in 2024, deepening your faith, spreading love, and living a purposeful life guided by the wisdom and insights from our shared journey. May each day bring you closer to the path of love, grace, and fulfillment God has prepared for you.

Day 1: Reflect on recent conversations. Identify instances where grace-filled responses could have improved communication.

Day 2: Practice active listening during face-to-face interactions. Pay attention to body language and respond with empathy and kindness.

Day 3: Engage in a discussion with a friend or family member. Prioritize understanding and compassion over proving a point.

Day 4: Before responding to a contentious online post, pause and rephrase your words to convey grace and respect.

Day 5: Meditate on Colossians 4:6. Consider how your speech can be seasoned with grace in various social settings.

Day 6: Volunteer at a local charity or community event. Use gentle words and actions to uplift those in need.

Day 7: Attend a church service or Bible study. Reflect on the sermon and discuss how to apply it to daily interactions with others.

Reflect on a recent conversation you had that left an impression on you, whether positive or negative. Consider the tone, words spoken, and overall atmosphere of the interaction. How did it align with the concept of a rich and black coffee, full of grace and seasoned with salt? Did your words stir up anger or turn away wrath, as described in Proverbs 15:1?

Think about a conversation you anticipate having shortly, whether with a friend, family member, colleague, or stranger. How can you apply the principles outlined in Colossians 4:6 to this upcoming interaction? Consider how you can infuse grace and wisdom into your words, guiding the conversation towards a positive outcome.

Create an action plan for incorporating grace-filled communication into your daily interactions. Identify specific strategies or techniques you can implement to ensure your conversations are seasoned with salt. How can you cultivate a habit of responding gently, even in challenging situations? Reflect on how this intentional approach aligns with your Christian values and can positively impact your relationships and interactions.

{124}

The 14th Pearl

Ignorance is "unique" to the "ill-literate and illiterate!" Disregard and disrespect are just the messengers who uttered the message. I'm just sayin'.

Welcome, beloved, to another blessed week in the grace of our Lord. As we embark on this journey together, let us open our hearts to receive the wisdom and guidance our Heavenly Father bestows. In our quest for spiritual enlightenment, we shall delve into the depths of understanding, drawing from this Pearl of Wisdom. At first glance, these words may appear cryptic, but let us unravel their profound significance. Ignorance, often misconstrued as a lack of knowledge, extends beyond mere illiteracy. It encompasses a state of mind unwilling to seek truth and understanding. It is a unique trait of those who refuse to engage with wisdom, whether due to a lack of education or a stubborn adherence to falsehoods.

Disregard and disrespect, the messengers of ignorance convey their message through their actions and words. They manifest in our interactions with others, reflecting our refusal to acknowledge their worth and dignity. When we disregard the inherent value of our fellow beings, we perpetuate ignorance and sow seeds of discord.

Let us turn to the Word of God to illuminate the essence of this pearl of wisdom. In the pursuit of knowledge and understanding, there exists a fundamental principle echoed throughout the scriptures—a principle encapsulated in the profound words of Proverbs 1:7: "The fear of the Lord is the beginning of knowledge, but fools despise wisdom and instruction." Here, the essence of humility and reverence is intricately woven into the fabric of understanding. To truly grasp the depths of knowledge, one must first acknowledge the sovereignty of God, recognizing His divine authority as the ultimate source of wisdom.

This notion is further illuminated in Colossians 3:8, where the apostle Paul implores believers to rid themselves of behaviors rooted in disrespect and disregard. Through a deliberate abandonment of anger, rage, malice, slander, and filthy language, we pave the way for spiritual growth and unity within the body of Christ. In rejecting these attitudes, we honor the inherent worth of others and affirm our commitment to embodying the teachings of Christ in our daily lives.

James 1:22 serves as a poignant reminder of the importance of active engagement with the Word of God. More than merely listening to its precepts is required; proper understanding is born out of a sincere desire to apply its teachings in our actions and attitudes. James urges us not to deceive ourselves by passively absorbing knowledge but to wholeheartedly embrace its transformative power.

Together, these scriptures paint a portrait of humility, reverence, and active obedience—a picture that beckons us to journey deeper into wisdom. As we navigate the complexities of life, may we heed the wisdom found within these sacred texts, ever mindful of the importance of humility, respect, and steadfast obedience to the Word of God.

In our quest for knowledge and understanding, we encounter various temptations and distractions that can lead us astray. The allure of worldly wisdom, coupled with the clamor of our desires, often pulls us away from the path of righteousness. However, the scriptures offer us a guiding light, illuminating the way forward amidst the darkness of ignorance and folly.

The Bible calls us to humility, reverence, and obedience, challenging us to align our hearts and minds with God's will. As we delve deeper into the Word, we face the stark reality of our limitations and shortcomings. Yet, acknowledging our need for divine guidance is precisely the key to unlocking the treasures of wisdom.

Moreover, the scriptures provide practical guidance on living out these principles daily. We are called to cast aside attitudes of anger and malice, replacing them with love and compassion. We are urged to guard our tongues from speaking ill of others, instead using our words to uplift and encourage. Above all, we are reminded of the importance of putting our faith into action and actively embodying the teachings of Christ in every aspect of our lives.

As we reflect on the wisdom contained within these scriptures, let us not merely be hearers of the Word but also doers. Let us cultivate a spirit of humility and reverence, surrendering our will to our Creator's divine wisdom. May we walk boldly in Christ's footsteps, guided by the light of His truth and the power of His love.

Key Points and Life Lessons:

- Humble Pursuit of Knowledge: We are called to approach wisdom with humility, recognizing our need for divine guidance.

- Respectful Interactions: Every encounter allows one to honor others' inherent worth, fostering unity and harmony.

- Living Out Truth: True wisdom is not confined to knowledge but manifests in righteous living and compassionate deeds.

Humility is the cornerstone of wisdom in our pursuit of knowledge. We are called to approach knowledge acquisition with a humble heart, recognizing our inherent limitations and the vastness of God's wisdom. This humility acknowledges our need for divine guidance, understanding that actual knowledge is not found solely in our own experience but is revealed to us through God's Word and Spirit.

Respectful interactions with others are integral to the Christian walk. Every encounter presents an opportunity to honor the inherent worth and dignity of those we encounter. Regardless of differences in background, opinion, or belief, we are called to treat others respectfully and kindly, recognizing each person as a beloved child of God. By fostering a spirit of unity and harmony in our interactions, we reflect the love of Christ to the world and contribute to building a community grounded in mutual respect and understanding. Living out truth entails more than mere intellectual knowledge; it requires a transformation of heart and mind.

True wisdom is not confined to accumulating facts or information but manifests in righteous living and compassionate deeds. As we align our lives with the truth of God's Word, we bear witness to His love and grace through our actions. This includes acts of kindness, justice, mercy, and compassion toward others, reflecting Christ's character in our daily lives. In living out the truth, we become vessels of God's light, shining brightly in a world that needs His love and redemption.

In today's fast-paced and interconnected world, ignorance often masquerades as certainty, and disregard for others permeates our discourse. However, the timeless truths encapsulated in the Scriptures offer a beacon of hope and guidance. For instance, in workplaces where diversity is celebrated, respecting colleagues of varying backgrounds echoes the biblical call to honor one another. Likewise, in social media, where opinions clash and civility wanes, embodying the principles of humility and respect can foster meaningful dialogue and understanding.

Imagine encountering a colleague who holds divergent views on a contentious issue. Rather than dismissing their perspective outright, strive to listen attentively and engage with empathy. Offer respect and dignity in your interactions, reflecting the love of Christ in all you do. As you embody the teachings of scripture, you contribute to a culture of mutual respect and understanding, transcending the barriers of ignorance and division.

As we conclude this week's lesson, may we carry the light of wisdom wherever we go, illuminating the darkness of ignorance with the truth of God's Word. Let us commit ourselves to the humble pursuit of knowledge, respectful interactions, and faithful obedience to the teachings of scripture. By embodying these principles daily, we witness the transformative power of Christ's love, drawing others closer to the source of all wisdom and understanding.

Much Love and Respect. Amen.

NaNa

As we continue our spiritual growth and enlightenment, let us reflect on the teachings we've received and actively engage in practices that deepen our understanding and transform our lives. Participating in these activities allows you to experience firsthand the profound impact of applying God's Word to every aspect of your life.

Through these intentional practices, may you discover new depths of faith, cultivate meaningful connections with others, and embody the love of Christ in all you do. Let us embrace this opportunity for growth and transformation, trusting in the guidance of the Holy Spirit as we journey together to pursue God's truth and wisdom.

Day 1: Engage in an online Bible study or podcast on humility and wisdom.

Day 2: Volunteer at a local shelter or community center, demonstrating respect and compassion for the needy.

Day 3: Host a small group discussion on fostering respectful dialogue in your social circles.

Day 4: Reflect on a passage of scripture related to humility and journal your insights.

Day 5: Share an uplifting message or scripture verse on social media, promoting positivity and encouragement.

Day 6: Attend a multicultural event or church service, celebrating the diversity of God's creation.

Day 7: Gather with fellow believers for fellowship and prayer, cultivating unity and mutual respect within the body of Christ.

Reflecting on NaNa's Pearl of Wisdom, "Ignorance is 'unique' to the illiterate!' Disregard & disrespect are just the 'messengers' that uttered the message," consider the following:

How have I experienced ignorance through lack of knowledge or a refusal to engage with truth and understanding?

My Cup Runneth Over

What messages have disregard and disrespect conveyed to me, and how have they influenced my perception of others and myself?

In what areas of my life do I need to actively seek knowledge, understanding, and wisdom to overcome ignorance?

How can I cultivate a mindset of openness and humility to receive guidance and wisdom from God and others?

What steps can I take this week to overcome ignorance and embrace a path of growth, enlightenment, and spiritual maturity?

Plan of Action:

- I commit to daily prayer and meditation, asking God for discernment and wisdom to recognize areas of ignorance in my life.

- I will regularly study scripture and other sources of spiritual insight to deepen my understanding of God's truth and His will for my life.

- Seek opportunities for learning and growth through books, courses, or conversations with knowledgeable mentors and peers.

- Practice humility and openness in my interactions, listening attentively and being willing to consider perspectives that differ from mine.

- I regularly reflect on my progress, celebrate moments of growth, learn from setbacks, and strive to understand truth and wisdom more deeply.

The 15th Pearl

Don't worry about things that are deemed "necessary evils"; they're there to motivate action. Make sure that the righteous are fighting the right fight in this spiritual warfare. The Saints who are in it will win.

The Righteous Fight in Spiritual Warfare

Welcome, beloved, to another blessed week in the presence of our Lord. Let us open our hearts and minds to receive the wisdom and guidance necessary for the journey ahead. As we dive deep into this pearl's depth, we draw strength from the sacred scriptures to illuminate our path and empower us for our battles.

In life's journey, we encounter what we might term "necessary evils" – challenges and tasks that push us out of our comfort zones and into action. These hurdles, though daunting, serve as catalysts for growth and development, motivating us to strive for betterment. However, amid these trials, it's crucial to discern the righteous battles worth fighting in our spiritual warfare. As saints, we're called to engage in these battles, aligning our efforts with God's will and fighting for justice and righteousness. By seeking guidance through prayer and scripture, we can ensure our actions are directed toward causes that honor God and advance His kingdom. With the assurance of victory through God's strength, we can courageously confront challenges, knowing that our perseverance in the right fights will ultimately lead to triumph.

Ephesians 6:12 (NIV): "For our struggle is not against flesh and blood, but against the rulers, against the authorities, against the powers of this dark world and against the spiritual forces of evil in the heavenly realms."

2 Timothy 4:7 (NIV): "I have fought the good fight, I have finished the race, I have kept the faith."

The essence of this Pearl of Wisdom resonates deeply within the core of our spiritual journey as believers. It beckons us to a profound understanding that transcends the mere surface of our existence. At its heart, it whispers a powerful truth: our lives are battlegrounds, arenas where the clash between light and darkness unfolds. On a literal plane, it implores us not to be consumed by the temporary hurdles and trials that pepper our path but to fix our gaze on righteousness, the compass guiding our every step. Yet, beyond the tangible, it speaks to the very essence of our being. It reminds us that our struggles are not confined to the material realm but are waged against the unseen forces of evil that seek to ensnare our souls. It calls us to discern with clarity and distinguish between that which uplifts and detracts from our spiritual ascent.

Metaphysically, it unveils a more profound truth: that our participation in this cosmic battle is not passive but active, demanding our unwavering dedication and enthusiasm. It underscores the necessity of channeling our energies toward noble endeavors rooted in the righteousness of our faith. It echoes the call for resilience and steadfastness, urging us to stand firm amidst the tumultuous waves of life's trials and tribulations. In this relentless pursuit of righteousness, we find victory and the essence of our souls' liberation. Supported by scriptures such as 1 Peter 5:8, which warns us to "Be alert and of sober mind. Your enemy the devil prowls around like a roaring lion looking for someone to devour," and James 4:7, which empowers us to "Submit yourselves, then, to God. Resist the devil, and he will flee from you," these Pearls of Wisdom becomes a mere piece of wisdom and a beacon guiding us through the darkness, illuminating the path toward spiritual triumph.

Key Points and Life Lessons:

- Our battles are spiritual, not merely physical.

- Focus on righteousness rather than worrying about necessary challenges.

- Perseverance and faithfulness are essential in spiritual warfare.

This Pearl of Wisdom urges us to prioritize our spiritual battles over worldly concerns. It teaches us that while challenges may be inevitable, our response to them defines our journey. We overcome obstacles and strengthen our faith by aligning our actions with righteousness and engaging in spiritual warfare.

In present-day life, this wisdom holds profound relevance. Losing sight of our spiritual journey is accessible in a world of distractions and temptations. However, by applying the principles of NaNa's Pearl and the accompanying scriptures, we can navigate life's challenges with clarity and purpose.

When confronted with unethical practices or challenging colleagues in the workplace, let us resist the temptation to succumb to worry. Instead, let us steadfastly uphold integrity and righteousness in all our actions, understanding that our actual adversaries lie within the spiritual realm. Likewise, amidst family discord or personal conflicts, let us not yield to despair. Instead, may we draw strength from our faith and persist in extending love and forgiveness, for we comprehend that our struggle transcends earthly conflicts; it is a battle against the spiritual darkness that seeks to divide and conquer.

As we conclude this week of spiritual empowerment and engagement, may we carry forward the lessons learned,d and the strength gained into the days ahead. Remember that our battles are not fought alone but with the assurance of victory through Christ, who strengthens us. As we walk in righteousness and faith, may we be ever mindful of NaNa's Pearl of Wisdom, guiding us in the righteous fight of spiritual warfare.

Glory and honor to God. Amen.

NaNa

Let us commit to daily practices that strengthen our resolve and deepen our faith. Each activity is designed to help us win in our spiritual warfare.

Day 1: Gather your loved ones for a Heavenly Creations Paint Night inspired by God's beautiful creation. Choose a theme centered around nature or biblical scenes, such as landscapes, animals, or stories from the Bible. Encourage participants to reflect on the magnificence of God's handiwork as they express themselves artistically through painting.

Day 2: Go on a Nature's Parables Scavenger Hunt with your family. Explore God's creation while discovering spiritual truths. Create a list of items that symbolize spiritual principles, such as a rock representing God's strength or a flower symbolizing His beauty. Along the way, discuss the spiritual significance of each finding, fostering a deeper connection to God's word and creation.

Day 3: Turn your kitchen into a sacred space for a Blessed Feast Cooking Challenge inspired by biblical feasts and meals. Choose recipes that evoke biblical imagery, such as unleavened bread, fish, or honey from the promised land. As you cook together, reflect on food's significance in scripture and God's provision's blessings.

Day 4: Engage in a Scripture Scavenger Hunt with your family, combining adventure with spiritual growth. Create a list of scriptures related to spiritual warfare and righteousness, such as Ephesians 6:10-18, 1 Peter 5:8-9, and James 4:7-8. Hide small cards with each scripture reference around your home or yard. Then, set out with your family to find and collect each scripture card. As you see each verse, take turns reading them aloud and discussing their significance in spiritual warfare and righteous living. Reflect on how these scriptures equip and empower believers to stand firm in their faith amidst challenges and trials. Finish by gathering together for a prayer time, asking God to strengthen and guide you in the spiritual battles you face. This activity fosters fun and meaningful dialogue, deepening your family's understanding of God's word and its relevance to daily life.

Day 5: Gather for a Faithful Fellowship Game Night Olympics with games that inspire faith and fellowship. Choose games encouraging teamwork, communication, and biblical knowledge, such as Bible trivia, charades with biblical themes, or a "fruits of the Spirit" relay race. Celebrate the joy of the Christian community as you bond through friendly competition and laughter.

Day 6: Divine Discoveries with your family through science experiments that reveal God's wonders and wisdom. Select experiments that showcase God's creative design and the order of the universe, such as studying the intricacies of a butterfly's wings or exploring the properties of water as a symbol of spiritual cleansing and renewal. Use each experiment as an opportunity to marvel at the greatness of our Creator and deepen your understanding of His divine handiwork.

Day 7: Set aside time as a family for a Grateful Hearts Journaling Session, reflecting on God's blessings and faithfulness. Begin by reading and meditating on scriptures of thanksgiving and praise, such as Psalm 100 or Psalm 136. Then, individually journal expressions of gratitude for God's goodness, provision, and love throughout the week. Encourage each family member to share their reflections, fostering a spirit of gratitude and worship in your home.

Reflecting on NaNa's Pearl of Wisdom, how do you discern between 'necessary evils' that motivate action and 'righteous' endeavors in our spiritual warfare? And in ensuring you are fighting the 'right' fight, how can you ensure that your actions are aligned with the will of God, trusting that as saints, we are not only in it but destined to emerge victorious?

The 16th Pearl

Change will come when the pain of staying the same is worse than the pain of change, But change MUST and WILL come.

The Winds of Change:

A Symphony of Transformation

This profound statement encapsulates the intricate dance between comfort and growth, familiarity and transformation, echoing through the corridors of human existence. At its core lies a deep understanding of the human condition and the dynamic interplay between our innate resistance to change and our relentless pursuit of growth.

While often met with resistance, change is essential for personal evolution and spiritual development. It is the crucible in which our character is refined, our resilience tested, and our true potential unlocked. The discomfort and challenges accompanying change serve as signposts on the path to self-discovery, guiding us toward greater self-awareness and fulfillment.

Moreover, change is not merely a temporary disruption but an intrinsic aspect of the human experience. It is woven into the fabric of existence itself, shaping the trajectory of our lives and propelling us towards our destinies. Embracing change requires courage, faith, and a willingness to surrender to the unknown.

This Pearl of Wisdom calls us to embrace change's inevitability and recognize its transformative power in our lives. It challenges us to let go of our attachments to the past and to step boldly into the future, trusting in the divine orchestration of our journey. For it is in the embrace of change that we find the most authentic expression of our humanity and the boundless potential of our souls, transcending the limitations of our perceived reality to soar amidst the infinite possibilities of existence.

In the grand orchestration of life, change emerges as the conductor, orchestrating movements of growth, renewal, and divine intervention. NaNa's Pearl of Wisdom extends a beckoning call, urging us to embrace the winds of change, for within their tumult lies the haunting melody of our destiny. This call is not arbitrary; it resonates with the divine whisper, nudging us towards greater heights of spiritual evolution and fulfillment.

"Behold, I am doing something new; now it springs forth, do you not perceive it? I will make a way in the wilderness and rivers in the desert." - **Isaiah 43:19** (ESV)

The desolate wilderness of our lives is not forsaken, for God promises to usher in a season of renewal and abundance. Here, amidst parched lands, He orchestrates a symphony of transformation, turning barren wastelands into fertile oases teeming with life. This verse is a clarion call to awaken from our slumber, to recognize the dawn of new beginnings amidst the shadows of despair.

"But they who wait for the Lord shall renew their strength; they shall mount up with wings like eagles; they shall run and not be weary; they shall walk and not faint." - **Isaiah 40:31** (ESV)

In the waiting, there is a divine renewal of strength. Like the majestic eagle soaring above storms, we are called to transcend the limitations of our circumstances. In the patient endurance of trials, we find our wings, enabling us to rise above adversity with unwavering faith and resilience. Here lies the promise of divine empowerment, granting us the endurance to persevere without faltering.

"Therefore, if anyone is in Christ, he is a new creation. The old has passed away; behold, the new has come." - **2 Corinthians 5:17** (ESV)

In Christ, the symphony of transformation reaches its crescendo. Here, amidst the ashes of the old, emerges the phoenix of the new—a rebirth of spirit and a renewal of soul. Through our union with Christ, we are liberated from the shackles of our past and equipped to embrace the limitless possibilities of our future. It is a call to shed the burdens of guilt and shame, for in Christ, we are adorned with the robes of righteousness, ready to embark on a journey of purpose and abundance.

NaNa's Pearl of Wisdom and the accompanying scriptures offer profound insights into the nature of change and its significance in our lives. In a world characterized by rapid upheaval and uncertainty, they serve as guiding beacons, illuminating the path toward personal and spiritual growth. By embracing change with faith and resilience, we can navigate life's challenges with grace and courage, knowing that God's plans for us are filled with hope and purpose.

In present-day life, these truths manifest in various scenarios. Consider a career transition where individuals may face fear and uncertainty. By trusting in God's plan and embracing the opportunity for growth, they can embark on a journey of self-discovery and fulfillment, confident that He has plans to prosper them. Similarly, in tumultuous relationship dynamics, individuals can renew their minds and align their actions with God's will. Doing so allows them to navigate relational challenges with wisdom and grace, fostering deeper connections and mutual understanding.

As we reflect upon the transformation symphony echoed in these sacred verses, let us heed the divine call to action. Let us embrace change as the harbinger of divine transformation, renewing our strength in adversity and embracing our new identity in Christ. Let us share the melody of transformation with others, embracing vulnerability as the fertile soil for growth and cultivating resilience in the face of life's storms. Ultimately, let us surrender control and trust in the divine orchestration of our lives, knowing that His plans for us are far greater than we could ever imagine.

In the depths of change, we discover that transformation is not merely a destination but a journey of surrender, resilience, and unwavering faith. It calls us to embrace the unknown, to dance in the shadows of uncertainty, and to trust in the divine guidance that leads us ever onward. And as we surrender to the symphony of change, we find ourselves swept up in its melody, carried aloft on wings of hope and possibility, towards the glorious crescendo of our destiny.

As we stand on the precipice of transformation, let us heed the call of the winds of change, knowing that within their tumult lies the promise of new beginnings, divine renewal, and boundless possibility. Let us embrace the symphony of transformation that echoes through our lives, knowing that we find the most genuine expression of our souls and the most profound revelation of God's love during change. So let us raise our voices in song, dance to the rhythm of change, and journey forth with hearts ablaze, knowing that in the symphony of transformation, we are forever changed, renewed, and embraced by the boundless grace of the Divine. Amen.

As we embark on this journey of self-discovery and spiritual growth, may we embrace change with faith and resilience, knowing that God's plans for us are filled with hope and purpose? May we embody the transformative power of His love through daily reflection and action, bringing about positive change in our lives and the world around us. Amen.

By His Love and Mercy

NaNa

By incorporating these daily activities into your life, you can embark on a transformative journey in 2024, deepening your faith, spreading love, and living a purposeful life guided by the wisdom and insights from our shared journey. May each day bring you closer to the path of love, grace, and fulfillment God has prepared for you.

Day 1: Digital Detox: Spend an hour disconnecting from digital distractions and meditating on change and renewal. Reflect on how embracing change can lead to personal growth and spiritual transformation.

Day 2: Gratitude Journaling: Write down three things you're grateful for and how they signify positive changes in your life. Cultivate a spirit of gratitude for the transformative blessings bestowed upon you.

Day 3: Acts of Kindness: Perform a random act of kindness for someone in need, embodying the transformative power of love and compassion. Recognize how small acts of kindness can positively change others and one's lives.

Day 4: Nature Walk: Take a leisurely walk in nature and contemplate the beauty of seasonal changes. Find solace in the natural rhythms of change, embracing them as a reflection of God's divine plan.

Day 5: Community Service: Volunteer at a local charity or organization that serves those undergoing significant life changes. Witness firsthand the transformative impact of community support and solidarity.

Day 6: Scripture Study: Delve deeper into the scriptures cited, seeking spiritual insights into the nature of change and transformation. Reflect on how the lessons can be applied to your life journey.

Day 7: Fellowship and Reflection: Gather with fellow believers for worship and reflection on the week's theme of change and transformation. Share personal insights and experiences, reaffirming your commitment to embracing God's plan for your life.

Consider the various facets of your life, relationships, and personal performance. Reflect on a specific area where you have hesitated to embrace change due to the fear of discomfort or uncertainty. How can you shift your perspective to recognize that change is inevitable and essential for growth and fulfillment?

How can you harness the discomfort of staying stagnant as a catalyst for embracing necessary changes in your life, relationships, and personal productivity? Describe concrete steps to overcome resistance to change and embrace the transformative journey ahead with courage, faith, and determination.

Closing Prayer

O Sovereign God. My Lord, Savior, Healer, and Redeemer, I praise you for the gift of life, love, and blended and extended family. More importantly, I thank you for blessing my transcending generations to be the "wind beneath my wings," freeing me from the confinement of procrastination and helping me to declare openly the affirmation of "who" I am and "whose" I am. I am your vessel, desiring to give honor to the "Potter" who yet molds me on "the Wheel."

I pray that as I make intercession for those You have placed in my life and the pathways of my journey on earth, You, O Lord, will continue to intercede for me, pleading my case for the forgiveness of my faults and sins of commission and omission.

I desire to have a positive and life-changing impact on everyone you have placed before me. Fortify me with a measure of wisdom, faith, unconditional love, and humility—seasoned with Holy Boldness—to declare your awesomeness and miraculous healing power; your plan of salvation and hope for the hopeless; and your Grace and yet abounding mercies to all with whom I encounter.

Anoint my loved ones with oil and bless them to walk circumspectly of their calling – that I, too, carry myself so as not to bring reproach upon Your name or Your people. May they continue to be "shelters" for the innocent ones who have been caught in the entrapments of life's various storms – and when they too are caught up in the storm – be their life raft; calm the seas, and let them walk upon the waters by faith, as you bid them to come.

I pray and petition that we be counted among those who enter the place you have prepared for a prepared people—our eternal resting place.

ALL GLORY and ALL HONOR BELONGS TO YOU, enthroned upon the highest heavens, reigning in majesty and splendor. You alone are worthy of all adoration and praise. Amen. Hallelujah! Amen.

Call To Action

Beloved, as we stand at the crossroads of change, let us heed the divine call to transformation. Let us cast aside our fears and doubts and embrace the winds of change with open hearts and minds. May we be vessels of divine renewal and empowerment, shining beacons of hope and inspiration in a world longing for transformation. In embracing change, we find the keys to unlock the doors of our destiny and fulfill the divine purpose for which we were created. Amen.

Additional Scriptures for Study:

- Ecclesiastes 3:1-8

- Isaiah 43:18-19

- 2 Corinthians 5:17

- Philippians 4:6-7

- Psalm 46:10

- Romans 8:28

- Romans 12:2

- Psalm 27:14

- Psalm 23:1

- Proverbs 3:5-6

- Isaiah 40:31

- Jeremiah 29:11

- Matthew 6:33

- Ephesians 2:10

- Galatians 6:9

- James 1:2-4

- Psalm 37:4

- Hebrews 11:1

- 1 Peter 5:7

- Matthew 11:28-30

- Revelation 21:4

Recommended Books for Reading:

"The Purpose Driven Life" by Rick Warren

"Embraced: 100 Devotions to Know God Is Holding You Close" by Lysa TerKeurst

"Transforming Your Thought Life: Christian Meditation in Focus" by Sarah Geringer

"The Road Less Traveled" by M. Scott Peck

"The Power of Now" by Eckhart Tolle

"Streams in the Desert" by L.B. Cowman

The book reports are provided for you in the appendix, which offer deeper insights into the themes and messages explored in each respective book, providing readers with additional resources for spiritual growth and understanding.

Although I "shun" most opportunities to "talk about myself," from my breach of birth, childhood memories and experiences, "coming-of-age" life lessons, affairs of the heart, and religious introduction to my Spiritual awakening and maturity, I can only define it as PURPOSE.

My memories and experiences being etched into my mind are often "replayed" like a movie series on a cellophane reel.

I became an avid reader at age 3. From then on, I have concluded that every experience, crossroad, and choice, regardless of the consequences, can be summed up as "working for my good." (See Romans 8:28: "And we know that all things work together for good to them that love God, to them who are the called according to His purpose.")

I am intensely interested in most things related to the "mind." In my post-high school education, I applied myself enthusiastically to my studies of Psychology and related courses: Social Psychology, Behavioral Psychology, Cultural Anthropology, and Transcendental Meditation.

To me, religion—or religious beliefs—are akin to psychological discourse: they affect one's thinking before influencing one's behavior or way of life.

My relationship as a spiritual being is an ongoing process in biblical studies and personal experiences of faith, divine "gifts" of enlightenment, prayer, and discernment.

As time and opportunities present themselves, I have been privileged to give testimonies relating to what I have personally experienced. The "PEARLS" are a result of inflections/or responses to personal, social, cultural, and historical events I have lived through.

The value placed on all these are like precious gems to me – for they have been processed like natural pearls, having been exposed to "living bacteria," protected by a "Covering" which has endured 'hardening' – that resulted in a "healed" mollusk. (I, too, have a "SHELL" that protects me from untoward elements.)

Appendix

"The Purpose Driven Life" by Rick Warren

"The Purpose Driven Life" by Rick Warren is a profound and impactful exploration of the fundamental question: What on earth am I here for? Through insightful reflections, practical advice, and biblical wisdom, Warren guides readers on self-discovery and spiritual growth, unveiling the purpose and meaning behind their existence.

The book is divided into 40 chapters, each addressing a different aspect of life's purpose. Warren emphasizes that everyone's journey is unique, yet all are interconnected by the overarching theme of God's plan and design for humanity. He asserts that discovering one's purpose begins with understanding and embracing God's intentions for our lives rather than seeking self-centered ambitions.

Warren delves into five essential purposes that form the foundation of a meaningful life: worship, fellowship, discipleship, ministry, and mission. He highlights the importance of cultivating a deep relationship with God through prayer, worship, and scripture study and fostering connections with others through genuine fellowship and community.

Throughout the book, Warren challenges readers to reflect on their priorities, values, and beliefs, urging them to align their lives with God's purposes. He emphasizes the significance of serving others and positively impacting the world, encouraging readers to use their unique talents and gifts to improve society.

One of the most compelling aspects of The Purpose Driven Life is Warren's ability to blend profound spiritual insights with practical guidance for everyday living. At the end of each chapter, he provides actionable steps and reflection questions, empowering readers to apply the book's principles to their lives.

Moreover, Warren's writing is deeply rooted in scripture, drawing on biblical passages and stories to illustrate his points and offer timeless wisdom. He seamlessly weaves together theology, psychology, and personal anecdotes to create a compelling narrative that resonates with readers of all backgrounds.

Overall, "The Purpose Driven Life" is a transformative and enlightening book that challenges readers to reevaluate their priorities, discover their unique purpose, and live intentionally in alignment with God's plan. It serves as a spiritual growth and fulfillment roadmap, guiding readers toward a life of meaning and eternal significance.

"Embraced: 100 Devotions to Know God Is Holding You Close" by Lysa TerKeurst

"Embraced: 100 Devotions to Know God Is Holding You Close" by Lysa TerKeurst is a soul-stirring journey into the comforting embrace of God's love and presence. Through a collection of 100 devotions, TerKeurst tenderly guides readers to experience the profound truth that no matter what trials or uncertainties they may face, they are held securely in the loving arms of their Heavenly Father.

Finding Comfort in God's Embrace:

TerKeurst's devotions offer solace and reassurance to those navigating life's challenges, reminding them they are never alone. Each devotion invites readers to draw near God, finding comfort in His unfailing love and presence. TerKeurst beautifully captures the essence of Psalm 139:9-10, which declares, "If I rise on the wings of the dawn, if I settle on the far side of the sea, even there your hand will guide me, your right hand will hold me fast." This verse is a poignant reminder that God's loving embrace surrounds us wherever we go.

Trusting in God's Faithfulness:

Throughout "Embraced," TerKeurst encourages readers to trust God's faithfulness, even amid life's uncertainties. She shares personal anecdotes and biblical insights to illustrate the unwavering nature of God's love and His commitment to His children. This echoes the words of Isaiah 41:10, where God promises, "So do not fear, for I am with you; do not be dismayed, for I am your God. I will strengthen, help, and uphold you with my righteous right hand." TerKeurst reminds readers that they can rest securely knowing God is faithful to His promises.

Experiencing Transformation Through God's Love:

"Embraced" is a collection of devotions and a transformative journey into deeper intimacy with God. TerKeurst invites readers to surrender their fears, doubts, and insecurities to the One who loves them unconditionally. Through heartfelt prayers and reflections, readers are encouraged to experience the transformative power of God's love in their lives. TerKeurst beautifully articulates, "When we open our hearts to God's love, we allow Him to transform us from the inside out." This sentiment resonates with the apostle Paul's words in Romans 12:2, urging believers to be transformed by renewing their minds.

Conclusion:

Lysa TerKeurst's "Embraced: 100 Devotions to Know God Is Holding You Close" is a poignant reminder of God's unshakeable love and presence in the lives of His children. Through heartfelt devotions and profound insights, TerKeurst invites readers to draw near God and experience His embrace's fullness. As readers journey through the pages of "Embraced," they are reminded of the profound truth that they are cherished, valued, and held securely in the arms of their Heavenly Father.

"Transforming Your Thought Life: Christian Meditation in Focus" by Sarah Geringer

In "Transforming Your Thought Life: Christian Meditation in Focus," author Sarah Geringer profoundly explores the power of Christian meditation to renew the mind and transform lives. Drawing from her own experiences and insights, Geringer offers practical guidance and biblical wisdom to help readers cultivate a more profound, intentional meditation practice rooted in the Christian faith.

Key Takeaways:

1. Understanding the Power of Thought: Geringer emphasizes the importance of recognizing the impact of our thoughts on our emotions, behaviors, and overall well-being. Acknowledging the power of our thought life allows readers to take responsibility for their mental and spiritual health.

2. Renewing the Mind with Scripture: Geringer highlights the transformative power of immersing oneself in Scripture through Christian meditation. By meditating on God's Word, readers can replace negative thought patterns with the truth of God's promises, leading to greater peace, joy, and spiritual growth.

3. The Practice of Stillness: Geringer emphasizes the significance of cultivating a habit of stillness and silence amid life's busyness. Through intentional quiet reflection and meditation, readers can create space to hear God's voice and experience His presence.

4. Overcoming Anxiety and Fear: Addressing everyday struggles such as anxiety and fear, Geringer offers practical strategies and biblical principles to help readers overcome negative thought patterns and find freedom in Christ. By surrendering their worries to God and meditating on His Word, readers can experience peace that transcends understanding.

5. Living with Purpose and Intention: Geringer challenges readers to live with purpose and intentionality, aligning their thoughts and actions with God's will for their lives. Through Christian meditation, readers can cultivate a deeper intimacy with God and discern His guidance for their journey.

Connection with Bible Verses:

1. Romans 12:2 - "Do not conform to the pattern of this world, but be transformed by the renewing of your mind. Then you will be able to test and approve what God's will is—his good, pleasing and perfect will." (NIV) - This verse resonates with the central theme of renewing the mind through Christian meditation and aligning one's thoughts with God's truth.

2. Psalm 46:10 - "Be still, and know that I am God; I will be exalted among the nations, I will be exalted in the earth" (NIV)—Geringer emphasizes the practice of stillness and silence in meditation, which is echoed in this verse. It reminds readers of the importance of quieting their hearts to hear God's voice.

3. Philippians 4:8 - "Finally, brothers and sisters, whatever is true, whatever is noble, whatever is right, whatever is pure,

whatever is lovely, whatever is admirable—if anything is excellent or praiseworthy—think about such things." (NIV) - This verse aligns with Geringer's encouragement to focus on positive, uplifting thoughts rooted in God's Word.

Conclusion:

"Transforming Your Thought Life: Christian Meditation in Focus" offers readers a transformative journey towards renewed minds and transformed lives. Through practical insights, biblical wisdom, and powerful meditation techniques, Sarah Geringer equips readers to overcome negative thought patterns, embrace God's truth, and live with purpose and intentionality. This book is a valuable resource for anyone seeking to deepen their spiritual walk and experience the life-changing power of Christian meditation.

"The Road Less Traveled" by M. Scott Peck

In "The Road Less Traveled" by M. Scott Peck, the author takes readers on a transformative journey toward self-discovery, growth, and spiritual fulfillment. Through insightful anecdotes, profound reflections, and practical advice, Peck challenges readers to confront the complexities of life with courage, honesty, and resilience. One of the major takeaways from this book is the importance of embracing discipline and responsibility as essential components of personal development and spiritual evolution. Peck emphasizes the necessity of facing and overcoming difficulties rather than avoiding them to achieve true fulfillment and inner peace. This theme resonates strongly with biblical principles, such as those found in James 1:2-4, which encourages perseverance in the face of trials, and Romans 5:3-5, which highlights the transformative power of endurance and character development through adversity. Furthermore, Peck's emphasis on the value of love as the foundation of meaningful relationships echoes the teachings of 1 Corinthians 13:4-7, which extols the virtues of patience, kindness, and selflessness in interpersonal connections. Overall, "The Road Less Traveled" is a timeless guide for navigating life's challenges with grace, wisdom, and spiritual insight, drawing upon biblical wisdom to illuminate the path toward true fulfillment and enlightenment.

Exploring "The Power of Now" by Eckhart Tolle Through a Spiritual Lens

"The Power of Now" by Eckhart Tolle is a transformative guide to spiritual awakening and living in the present moment. Through profound insights and practical wisdom, Tolle invites readers to transcend the confines of the egoic mind and embrace the eternal now as the gateway to inner peace and enlightenment. As we delve into the depths of Tolle's teachings, we discover parallels with timeless truths found in the Bible, illuminating the path to spiritual growth and understanding.

Living in the Present Moment:

Tolle emphasizes the importance of mindfulness and presence, urging readers to let go of past regrets and future anxieties and fully immerse themselves in the present moment. This resonates deeply with the teachings of Jesus, who frequently emphasized the value of living in the now. In Matthew 6:34, Jesus says, "Therefore do not worry about tomorrow, for tomorrow will worry about itself. Each day has enough trouble of its own." This verse reminds us of the futility of dwelling on the future and the necessity of embracing the present moment with faith and trust in God's providence.

Overcoming the Ego:

Central to Tolle's teachings is the concept of ego identification and its role in human suffering. He encourages readers to disidentify from the egoic mind and find liberation in pure awareness. This mirrors the biblical injunction to crucify the ego and live in alignment with the Spirit. Galatians 2:20 declares, "I have been crucified with Christ, and I no longer live, but Christ lives in me. The life I now live in the body, I live by faith in the Son of God, who loved and gave himself for me." This verse speaks to the transformative power of surrendering the ego and allowing the divine presence to guide our lives.

Embracing Stillness and Silence:

Tolle emphasizes the importance of stillness and silence as gateways to inner peace and spiritual awakening. By quieting the constant chatter of the mind, we can connect with the deeper dimensions of our being and experience the presence of God. Psalm 46:10 echoes this sentiment, proclaiming, "Be still, and know that I am God; I will be exalted among the nations, I will be exalted in the earth." This verse reminds us of the sacredness of stillness and the divine presence that awaits us in moments of quiet contemplation.

Finding Joy in Being:

Tolle's message invites us to find joy and fulfillment in simply being rather than incessantly striving for external validation or future goals. This aligns with Jesus' teaching on the abundant life found in Him. John 10:10 proclaims, "The thief comes only to steal and kill and destroy; I have come that they may have life, and have it to the full." Jesus invites us to experience the richness of life by abiding in Him and embracing the present moment with gratitude and joy.

Conclusion:

Eckhart Tolle's "The Power of Now" offers profound insights into the nature of consciousness and the path to spiritual awakening. Through its teachings, readers are invited to transcend the limitations of the egoic mind and discover the eternal presence of God within themselves. As we journey through Tolle's words, we are reminded of the timeless truths found in the Bible, which serve as guiding lights on the path to inner peace, fulfillment, and union with the Divine.

"Streams in the Desert" by L.B. Cowman Through a Spiritual Lens

L.B. Cowman's "Streams in the Desert" is a timeless classic that offers spiritual nourishment and encouragement to weary souls traversing life's desert landscapes. Cowman draws upon biblical truths and personal anecdotes through daily devotions and reflections to sustain the journey, reminding readers of the ever-flowing streams of God's grace, mercy, and presence.

Finding Refreshment in the Desert:

Cowman's devotions provide hope and renewal in life's parched wilderness. Drawing upon imagery from the biblical metaphor of streams in the desert, Cowman encourages readers to seek out the life-giving waters of God's Word and presence. Psalm 42:1-2 beautifully captures this longing for spiritual refreshment, declaring, "As the deer pants for streams of water, so my soul pants for you, my God. My soul thirsts for God, for the living God. When can I go and meet with God?" Cowman's devotions echo this sentiment, inviting readers to come and drink deeply from the wellsprings of God's love and grace.

Trusting in God's Provision:

Throughout "Streams in the Desert," Cowman emphasizes the importance of trusting God's provision, even during life's trials and hardships. Drawing upon biblical narratives of God's faithfulness to His people, Cowman reminds readers that God is a faithful provider who meets our needs according to His riches in glory.

Philippians 4:19 reaffirms this: "And my God will meet all your needs according to the riches of his glory in Christ Jesus." Cowman's devotions serve as poignant reminders that God's provision never fails, even in the desert seasons of life.

Finding Strength in Surrender:

Cowman's devotions also explore the theme of surrender and submission to God's will, even when it leads through rugged and uncertain terrain. Drawing upon biblical examples of surrender, such as Jesus' prayer in the Garden of Gethsemane, Cowman encourages readers to yield their wills to God's perfect plan. Matthew 26:39 records Jesus' prayer, "Yet not as I will, but as you will." This profound surrender is a model for believers facing their trials and challenges. Cowman's devotions remind readers that true strength is surrendering to God's will and trusting His wisdom and goodness.

Experiencing Growth Through Trials:

"Streams in the Desert" also delves into the transformative power of trials and hardships in shaping our character and faith. Drawing upon the apostle Paul's words in Romans 5:3-4, Cowman writes, "Not only so, but we also glory in our sufferings, because we know that suffering produces perseverance; perseverance, character; and character, hope." Cowman's devotions encourage readers to embrace their trials as opportunities for growth and refinement, trusting that God is working all things together for their good.

Conclusion:

"Streams in the Desert" by L.B. Cowman is a timeless treasure trove of spiritual wisdom and encouragement. Through its daily devotions and reflections, Cowman invites readers to journey deeper into the heart of God, finding sustenance and refreshment amid life's desert places. As readers immerse themselves in the pages of "Streams in the Desert," they are reminded of the unchanging faithfulness of God, the transformative power of surrender, and the profound beauty of growth through trials. Indeed, this book is a source of inspiration and hope for all who traverse life's wildernesses.